# CYCLING
# *without*
# TRAFFIC:

## SOUTHWEST

### John Price

## DIAL
## HOUSE

First published 1996

ISBN  0 7110 2448 0

All rights reserved. No part of this book may be reproduced or transmitted in any form or by any means, electronic or mechanical, including photocopying, recording or by any information storage and retrieval system, without permission from the Publisher in writing.

© John Price 1996

Published by Dial House

an imprint of Ian Allan Ltd,
Terminal House, Station Approach, Shepperton,
Surrey TW17 8AS. Printed by Ian Allan Printing Ltd,
Coombelands House, Coombelands Lane, Addlestone,
Surrey KT15 1HY.

These pages are the result of a summer spent exploring the counties of the South West of England and discovering the best places for quiet, relaxed and traffic-free cycling. My cycle computer tells me that I have cycled 389 miles over these last five months. I have discovered old railway lines and canal towpaths; I have cycled in deep forest and across high moorland; I have cycled Roman roads and prehistoric trackways.

This book is written for 'potterers' — people who wish to spend a relaxing day cycling at no particular pace. It is also written with the family in mind who may be planning to take a holiday in the South West region. The book describes 30 rides in detail and contains a host of other information on cycling opportunities in the area; places of interest close to the rides; addresses of authorities and organisations that can provide further information.

As cyclists we live in very exciting times. The UK has spent the last half century as the Luddite of Europe with only a fraction of the cycle paths of countries like France, Germany and Holland. But now, thanks to the Millennium Fund, Sustrans' plan for a 6,500-mile National Cycle Network is really rolling forward, and the next few years should see significant progress. So, we can bask in the knowledge that we are about to enter a golden age of enlightenment, but in the meantime there is already a surprising amount of extremely pleasant cycling just waiting to be discovered with the help of this book.

## Acknowledgements

All photographs are by the author with the exception of those supplied by the AA Photo Library on pages 18 (inset), 26, 31, 37, 44, 50, 62 and 66 and Alan C. Butcher on page 60.

The John Betjeman quotation on page 98 is reproduced with permission of John Murray Publishers Ltd.

Maps by RS Illustrations, Liss, Hants.

*Below:* North Down Plantation.

The aim of this book is to supply the ideas and information that a family needs to enjoy a day out in the countryside with completely safe cycling. Information has been obtained from many sources including Sustrans, the British Waterways Board, the Forestry Commission, the Dartmoor National Park Authority and county and district councils. Cycling opportunities can be broken down into the following categories:

## Dismantled Railways

These are ideal for family cycling as they are usually flat, ideally surfaced and well-drained. Some are almost intact like the Plym Valley Trail, and virtually uninterrupted cycling can be enjoyed for many miles, but others have had their bridges removed which can make a dismantled railway ride frustratingly hard work. If you study an Ordnance Survey Landranger or Pathfinder map you will see many dismantled railway routes that could have been made into cycle trails — it would have been a ready-made national cycle network. The loss of these routes, largely due to the 'Beeching cuts', was such a short-sighted policy. Many of them have now been built on, or had their course extinguished beyond recovery.

## Canal Towpaths

Canal towpaths are excellent for cycling as they provide a flat route, there is always something going on in a peaceful sort of way, and there is an abundance of flora and fauna. The number of canals in the South West is very limited and there are basically only two of note — the Kennet and Avon and the Bridgwater and Taunton. Cycling on these is fully covered in the main part of this book, with three suggested rides on the former and two on the latter. Cycling is well catered for on the Kennet and Avon Canal, with cycling continuously possible from Froxfield Bridge at Hungerford through to Bath — a distance of 37 miles with a towpath surface that in many places has been specifically surfaced for cycling and consequently in the summer

months is extremely popular along certain stretches. On the other hand you will find the Bridgwater and Taunton towpath more variable with some parts unsurfaced and quite hard work, but it is so very quiet and consequently has a particular charm all of its own. A free permit is currently required for cycling these towpaths and details of how to get one are contained in the route descriptions of the five canal routes. The only other canal that is potentially cycleable is the Grand Western at Tiverton. Sadly, cycling is prohibited there — although I did see evidence of tyre tracks on the surface! This is most unfortunate as there are painfully few opportunities for traffic-free cycling in Devon and the towpath would make an ideal 11-mile route through some glorious countryside.

## Forestry Commission Land

Cycling is encouraged on most tracts of land owned or managed by the Forestry Commission. In the South West of England we are fortunate to have the New Forest where there are many miles of possible traffic-free cycling opportunities on good forestry roads, with a number of waymarked trails. Similarly the Dartmoor National Park provides cycling opportunities of a more rugged nature. The section on Forestry Commission land and National Parks provides further information.

## Cycling on Quiet Roads and Rights of Way

I often prefer to cycle part of a route on quiet country roads as they take you through our beautiful villages, which a railway or canal-based route might very well bypass. Some of the routes in this book are based on a traffic-free route but suggest a return leg on a quiet country lane. If you wish to enjoy the increased range of cycling that can be obtained by considering quiet lanes then many of the county and district councils produce recommended routes in their own areas. Examples are the Sticklepath Cycle Route in Devon, and the Wiltshire Cycleway. Details of many of these routes and points of contact for more information are contained

*Above:* Plenty of interest at Pewsey Wharf

in the chapter 'Routes Described in Local Authority Leaflets'. Alternatively, if you enjoy maps then why not plan a route for yourself. An Ordnance Survey Landranger map is the best for this. It will not take you much time to learn how to identify which of the 'yellow' roads are best for cycling. One fairly serious shortcoming of Ordnance Survey maps is the situation with 'white' roads. These are roads or tracks where it is impossible to tell from the map whether the public has access or not. Thankfully, the Ordnance Survey are just starting to make the first tentative steps to correct this on Pathfinder Series maps.

Finally, you can of course cycle on bridleways (but you must give way to horseriders and pedestrians), Roads Used as Public Paths (RUPPs) and Byways Open to All Traffic (BOATs). Although traffic may be free to use the latter classifications, it is fairly rare to encounter a vehicle, but the surface can be expected to be variable. The incidence of these rights of way that are usable by cyclists varies considerably from county to county. Wiltshire is one particular county which is especially suitable for cycling of this type with many miles of traffic-free cycling opportunities.

## The National Cycle Network

The completion of a National Cycle Network has been the aim of Sustrans for 15 years and this project has recently received a tremendous boost by obtaining funding of £42.5 million from the Millennium Commission. Sustrans plans to complete the first 2,500 miles by Easter 2000 at a cost of £183 million, with the remaining 4,000 miles due to be completed by 2005. Although the project is led by Sustrans, it is a partnership with over 400 local authorities and land-owning bodies, government departments and specialist and local interest groups. It will consist of approximately 50% traffic-free sections with the remainder on segregated or traffic-calmed roads. A fundamental design aim is that the whole network will be safe for use by a sensible, unsupervised 12 year old. You will see, during the lifetime of this book, the network developing. Some of it will follow the same routes, and some will no doubt cross the routes. Whatever happens, the network is a major step forward and will be a tremendous contribution to the cycling amenities of this country.

# SOUTHWEST AREA

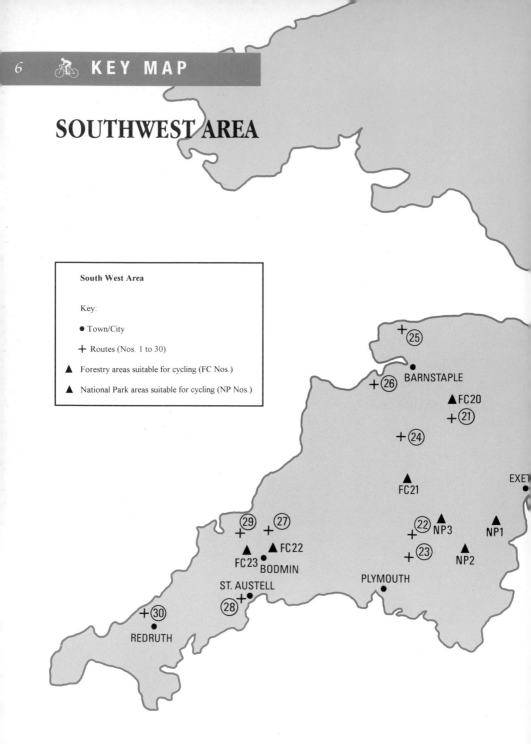

South West Area

Key:

● Town/City

+ Routes (Nos. 1 to 30)

▲ Forestry areas suitable for cycling (FC Nos.)

▲ National Park areas suitable for cycling (NP Nos.)

+ ㉕

+ ㉖ BARNSTAPLE

▲FC20

+ ㉑

+ ㉔

▲ FC21

EXE

+ ㉒ NP3 ▲ NP1 ▲

+ ㉙ + ㉗

▲ FC22

FC23 BODMIN

+ ㉓ NP2 ▲

PLYMOUTH

ST. AUSTELL

+ ㉘

+ ㉚

REDRUTH

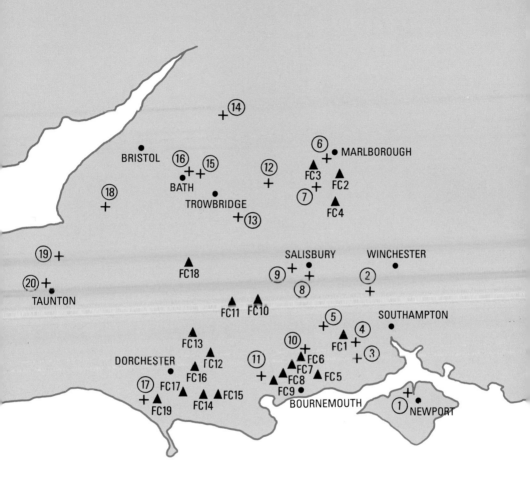

BRISTOL

⑯ ⑮

BATH

⑱

TROWBRIDGE

⑭

⑫

⑥ MARLBOROUGH

FC3

FC2

⑦

FC4

⑬

⑲

SALISBURY    WINCHESTER

FC18

⑨

⑧

②

FC11  FC10

TAUNTON

⑳

⑤

SOUTHAMPTON

⑩

FC1

④

③

DORCHESTER

FC13

⑪

FC6

FC12

FC16

FC7

FC8  FC5

⑰  FC17

FC9

FC19  FC14  FC15

BOURNEMOUTH

①  NEWPORT

## The Bicycle

Broadly there are four basic types of bike available in the shops today that would be suitable for the potterer. Starting with the least sophisticated there is the traditional sit-up-and-beg three-speed roadster, favoured by vicars and students in Oxford and Cambridge. Then there is the touring bike, characterised by its drop handlebars and racks for carrying panniers. The mountain bike has in recent years become ever more popular because of its ability to go anywhere. Finally, there is the hybrid which looks like a mountain bike but has a smaller diameter and thinner tyres so you get the advantage of the robustness of a mountain bike combined with greater speed. All of the rides classified as easy in this book could be undertaken on all four types, but the moderate or demanding ones would make a mountain or hybrid desirable. If you are not certain which cycle you wish to buy, try hiring one first. Then when you have tried cycling and you discover that you are enjoying it, go to a small shop that specialises in cycling and seek advice.

## Helmet and Headgear

The potterer should wear a helmet if he or she is able to and should try to ensure that children wear one. Having said that, even the modern lightweight ventilated ones are very uncomfortable and inconvenient on a hot day when sweat drips into your eyes. If you really cannot bring yourself to wear a helmet at certain times, comfort yourself with the thought that the health and fitness benefits of cycling are considerably greater than the actual chance of a serious head injury. As far as children are concerned the risk of a serious head injury is only about a third of the risk of a child experiencing a head injury from climbing or jumping. Nevertheless, helmets offer a limited but significant amount of protection to the skull and brain if you fall off and hit your head on the ground. If you are not wearing a helmet in cold weather, you should wear a hat as it will save a significant amount of heat loss.

## Clothes

To wear or not to wear a pair of those infamous brightly coloured, body-hugging lycra cycling shorts for the first time is a big decision in the potterer's life. On the one hand they are a trifle over the top for pottering, and they show up all bulges, but they can be a real blessing. Shorts wear well, do not have seams in the wrong places and are lined with chamois which sticks to your skin and prevents abrasion. Tracksuit trousers or jogging suits are a good alternative but they need to be fairly tight fitting. There are specialist cycling tracksuits which have zip legs and high backs but ordinary tracksuit bottoms should suffice. Jeans are not a particularly good idea. They have large seams in the wrong places, are too stiff, and are cold when wet.

One of the least practical items for day-long rides are cycle clips. If you like to wear ordinary trousers and want to keep your self-respect by not tucking your trousers into your navy blue socks, then turn up the trouser leg a few inches.

On the upper half of the body it is best to follow the well-established layer principle, taking with you several layers of clothing rather than a single thick item, and peeling off or putting on as required.

As far as weather is concerned, it is very advisable to listen to a weather forecast before you decide to go cycling and that way you can avoid the worst soaking. If you do cycle in the rain, no matter what you wear, you will find yourself getting clammy and probably wet anyway, due to the waterproof garment not 'breathing' fast enough to rid the garment of perspiration, despite the claims of many manufacturers. The old-fashioned cape can be very good as it allows plenty of air circulation. If you take waterproofs, you will need to consider what

*Right:* Leaving Bridgwater

to carry them in. A rucksack is feasible, but a better idea is a set of front or rear panniers, with the latter probably being the best. These avoid a sweaty back and have a low centre of gravity. If you think big and go for a large set of panniers, these could suffice for the whole family.

## Footwear

There are now sophisticated pedal and shoe systems which attach the shoe to the pedal. The shoe has a plate that locates into the pedal and will release from the pedal by twisting the foot sideways. But they are a bit specialist for the potterer and for the purposes of this book, trainers are likely to be the best bet.

## What to Take

There is a minimal amount of kit that you need to take to stand you in good stead for most eventualities. The biggest worry is, of course, a puncture. To counter this you should ensure that you carry a pump with flexible connectors suitable for the range of tyre valves that you and your group may be using. I always carry both a puncture repair kit (the tapered edge patches are best) and a spare inner tube, on the grounds that if you are unable to repair a flat tyre your day out will be ruined. To accompany these, a set of three tyre levers are essential and an adjustable spanner with a capacity of up to about $1\frac{1}{2}$in. In the heat of summer it is important to remember to take sufficient drink to last you all day, so that you avoid

becoming dehydrated. You should also consider the best way to carry this guide book, or your map. You could use a handlebar-mounted bag, which often has a clear pocket on top, or obtain a handlebar map carrier, which is rare but very practical. Alternatively, you could use a walkers' map carrier, slung over your back. This sounds unlikely, but works quite well in practice. The following list includes the items a wise family should consider taking on a cycle ride:

- A waterproof
- A pump with appropriate connectors
- A puncture repair kit
- A spare inner tube
- A set of tyre levers
- An adjustable spanner
- A small screwdriver
- A spray can of cycle oil
- Spare jumpers
- Gloves (for winter, spring and autumn)
- A lock
- A rag or some 'wipes' to clean your hands after a repair
- A cycle bottle and carrier
- A map carrier or equivalent
- A small rucksack or pannier bag

Finally, the instructions given in the rides are recorded at specific distances. An inexpensive cycle computer would therefore be a useful aid.

This is not a book on bicycle maintenance but it is important to carry out certain checks before a ride. Checking for faults after a ride is even better as it will mean that you are much more likely to have the time to sort the problem out properly. This section concentrates on safety-critical checks which can be divided into three categories:

## Brake Checks

Squeeze the brake lever and check that the brake blocks touch the rim after moving the lever between 1cm and 2cm from the rest position. If less, that is OK provided the rim does not rub against the block making your cycling hard work. If the movement is greater than 2cm then the brakes need adjusting. Brake cables tend to deteriorate through neglect so these need to be inspected regularly. If the cable is frayed or seriously rusty it should be replaced immediately. Inspect brake blocks and ensure that there is plenty of material left, indicated by the depth of the water-dispersing grooves. Better quality blocks have indicator lines which show the maximum wear limit. One of the most common and annoying problems that occurs with cycle brake blocks is squealing. This is easily solved in most cases by repositioning the blocks so that they take up a slightly 'tow-in' position.

## Tyre Checks

The rides in this book are not particularly demanding so the requirement is to have tyres which are properly inflated and have a full coverage of tread with no damaged sections. Mountain bike tyres will perform best if their pressure is varied according to anticipated use. Optimum grip for off-road use requires a lower pressure than minimum rolling resistance when on-road. Typical pressures for off- and on-road conditions are 40psi and 65psi respectively. If you do not possess a pressure gauge then squeeze the tyre sides. You should be able to press your thumb about 5mm into the side of the tyre. Inspect the tyre for adequacy of tread all around the circumference and for cuts in the sidewall and replace if there are any shortcomings.

## Wheel Tightness Check

Many modern bikes now have their wheels secured by quick release levers. These are extremely convenient and effective, but it is very important to ensure that they are correctly tightened, because failure to do so could be the cause of a very nasty accident. A correctly closed quick release lever will curve in toward the wheel when tightened and the annotation 'closed' should be seen on the lever. In principle it is a cam device and provided it is tightened with enough force to leave a slight imprint on your hand, it will not come open on its own.

After a ride ensure your bike is thoroughly cleaned, checked and lubricated. Any problems should be rectified by a competent mechanic. Doing this after a ride should ensure that you take action in time for your next outing. Cycle shops usually require a few days to complete repairs and it is unfair to turn up and expect the mechanic to fix a problem there and then.

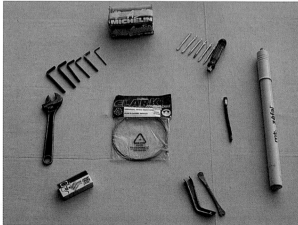

*Bicycle maintenance and mending a puncture.*

# Mending a Puncture on a Ride

The first observation to make here is that this will be a very unlikely occurrence as you will be carrying a spare tube (I often carry two). It is surprising how soon you can become chilled and your will-power starts to go if you stop to repair a puncture on a cold day. You will need to have with you:

- a puncture outfit
- tyre levers
- an adjustable spanner if you do not have quick-release levers
- a pump

NB If you are merely changing the tube, follow Instructions 1, 2, 3, 7, 10, 11 and 12.

1. Undo the wheel nuts. Release the brake cable if necessary, to enable the tyre to pass between the brake blocks.

2. Remove the tyre from the rim using levers only if unavoidable — many mountain bike tyres can be removed without the use of levers and this is preferable to avoid the risk of pinching the tube and causing additional holes. If using levers insert them about 80mm apart and push them down together. Then insert the third lever and push it down. Remove the middle one and edge around the tyre until you can release the remaining amount of tyre by hand.

3. Remove the dust cap and valve-securing nut and push the valve through the rim and then gently pull the tube out of the tyre.

4. Inflate the tube sufficiently to locate the puncture. Pass the tube close to your ear or lips to locate the escape of air. Mark the position of the puncture with a cross using the small crayon from the puncture repair outfit, or alternatively gently insert a small pin into the puncture.

5. Let the air out of the tyre and sandpaper the area vigorously to clean and roughen it. Select the minimum size patch necessary for the repair.

6. Spread a thin layer of glue over an area slightly larger than the proposed patch and allow to dry for 5min.

7. While waiting for the glue to dry, check the tyre for the cause of the puncture and remove it. If you are unable to find a cause, check that the spokes are not protruding through the rim and rim tape. You should be able to use the distance of the puncture from the valve to guide you to the cause.

8. Remove the foil from the patch and apply to the tyre, pressing down firmly all over. Pinch the patch to split the backing paper and gently peel off — this minimises the chance of lifting the edge of the patch. Dust the area with some dusted chalk or talcum powder.

9. Inflate the tyre sufficiently for a test. Carefully check for further punctures — they often come in twos and threes — then deflate.

10. Place the tube inside the tyre and insert the valve through the hole in the rim. Inflate with a very low pressure to prevent 'pinching' of the tube. Ensure the tube is completely inside the tyre and then gently ease the tyre back inside the rim. Use the palms of your hands if possible to minimise the chance of a pinch, using the levers only if absolutely necessary. If using levers, double check that there is no chance of pinching the tube between lever and rim.

11. Fully reinflate the tyre with a pressure appropriate to road or off-road use. Replace the valve-securing nut and dust cap. Check that the cover is positioned correctly by spinning the wheel, and deflate and re-position if necessary.

12. Place the wheel into the frame of the bike and secure the nuts tightly. Check that the wheel is correctly positioned by spinning it and adjusting if necessary. Reconnect the brake cable and test the brakes.

Escaping from our towns and cities to go walking is easy. We gather up our boots and rucksack, climb in our cars or on the bus and just go. Cycling requires a little more planning. Bikes need a rack for transport by car and you are not permitted to take them on the bus, so the whole idea needs more careful thought. We need to consider exactly how we are going to make our great escape from the pressures of city or town life to the tranquil pleasures of cycling in the country. The first means of escape is by the bike itself, but the chances of escaping from the town or city without dangerous exposure to heavy traffic is unlikely, until the National Cycle Network makes significant progress.

## Use of the Railway

Without doubt, the best way to travel to the start of a ride is by rail and let the train take the strain. But this is easier said than done. The position with regard to cycles on trains is complicated, changes regularly and depends on the region in which you wish to travel. With the impending break-up of the rail network the situation could very well get worse. For example, on many suburban electric trains in Hampshire it is currently possible for your cycle to travel in the guard's van with no advance notice and no charge, provided you are sensible and avoid rush hours. With trains with a small or no guard's van, where space is very limited and often only one cycle per carriage is possible, an advance booking is necessary and a small charge is levied. Suburban diesel Sprinter units and main line Inter-City 125 trains fall into this category.

If you are considering transporting your bike by rail, the most reliable advice that can be given is to contact your local railway information office as early as possible. If you do decide to use the train, make sure that you are on the platform in good time and report to the guard as soon as possible. It is best to wait three-quarters of the way towards the back end of the platform to spot the guard's van as it passes. With luck you will be seen and the doors will be opened. Prepare to load and unload your cycles yourself and be willing to move quickly. It is wise to tie a label on to your machine stating your name and destination. You should be most careful on Sundays as it is track maintenance day and it is important to ensure that the train will be running both ways without interruption. If a section of track is under maintenance, then buses are used to transport passengers and these are not permitted to carry cycles.

## Transport by Car

If, like many of us, you are not lucky enough to be close to a railway station, you have only one way to get to the start of these rides, and that is to use a car. It is possible to take your bike inside the car, if you remove one or more wheels, but that probably limits the number of cycles to be taken to just one. There is really no alternative other than to consider a cycle rack. There are two basic ways of carrying a bike: a rear-mounted carrier, and on the roof.

The rear-mounted carrier is probably the least expensive method, but you are generally limited to two bikes, sometimes three. The bikes mount sideways across the rear of the car, and the one big advantage is that you can see them during your journey. However, there is a tendency to make the car tail heavy, and you must ensure that your rear number plate is not covered or you will be committing an offence. There are also regulations restricting how much your 'payload' can protrude over your rear lights. That is not to say that these carriers are not a good idea, as they provide a cost-effective solution, but it is important that you check and consider these things before you part with your hard-earned cash.

The other alternative is to carry the bikes on the roof. You can strap them down with bungees on top of a roof-rack in which case they will quickly become scratched. The best but most expensive solution is to purchase roof bars and special cycle carriers that clamp to them. Without doubt, the best type of roof-bar-mounted cycle carrier is the type that secures the wheels in a channel that runs the length of the bike, and also clamps the diagonal member of the frame. These clamps are lockable and enable you to lock your bikes to the car. I have used one of these on a small Rover Metro and have found the arrangement satisfactory for carrying as many as four bikes. Most car manufacturers have roof bars and matching cycle carriers available as part of their accessory range. It is probable that buying equipment specifically matched to your car will generally provide the best, if not the cheapest solution, although versions for multi-application are widely available from car accessory shops.

Having firmly supported the advantages of roof bar carriers, there is also one disadvantage to be noted as I found to my cost in the lovely county town of Taunton, on an otherwise idyllic day in August. It is very easy to forget momentarily that there are cycles on the roof when entering car parks with restricted headroom, and this I duly did. Not only are many multi-storey car parks equipped with horizontal bars seemingly designed to cause maximum damage to cycles on the roof, but so, ironically, are many of the car parks specifically provided for many of the rides in this book. You will need to be vigilant if you use a roof-bar carrier.

**ROUTE 1**
THE NEWPORT TO COWES
CYCLEWAY

COWES

River Medina

1

2

3

Dodnor Creek

4

5

NEWPORT

N

# THE NEWPORT TO COWES CYCLEWAY

*...For groves of pine on either hand,
To break the blast of winter, stand;
And further on, the hoary Channel
Tumbles a billow on chalk and
sand;...*

Alfred Lord Tennyson from lines addressed to
the Rev F. D. Maurice in 1854

There are plenty of off-road cycling
opportunities on the Isle of Wight, but the
problem from the family cycling point of view is
that the island is essentially a hilly place. The
island council publish a very good set of four
mountain bike rides — details in the chapter on
'Routes Described in Local Authority Leaflets' —
but these are a little arduous for a family with
young children. Instead, I have decided to
recommend from a family viewpoint a short flat
ride that follows the old railway line from Cowes
to Newport. I took the ferry from Portsmouth
to Fishbourne, and then crossed the River
Medina from East to West Cowes via the floating
bridge, and started the ride from there. The
cycleway is very well signposted from both
Newport and Cowes, so you should have little
trouble finding your way to it.

**Background and Places of Interest**

●**The Isle of Wight**
The island is, geologically speaking, a most
interesting place. There are the Wealden
Clays which were formed in the Cretaceous
period by deposits from a large river and are
a prime site for dinosaur remains. There is
the Blue Slipper clay which, sandwiched
between greensands, results in significant
landslips as seen at Blackgang and
Luccombe. The central ridge that dominates
the island is chalk that was formed from
remains of microscopic sea creatures. North
of the central ridge are the soft rocks
characterised by the golden cliffs of Gurnard
and the famous and spectacular coloured
sand cliffs of Alum Bay. The 'ups and downs'

of the island — which make less than ideal cycling — were formed about 40 million years ago by the major upheavals and folding and buckling of rock strata that produced most of Europe's mountain ranges. The Ice Ages are responsible for the shape of the island that exists today except for a ridge that connected it to Dorset which was finally eroded by the sea about 7,000 years ago.

## ● Osborne House

Situated near East Cowes, Osborne House was built for Queen Victoria and Prince Albert between 1845 and 1851. The Italian-style villa was a place the couple loved and it was described by Queen Victoria as 'a Place of one's own, quiet and retired'. A visit there reveals so much about Victorian life: the drawing room with its marble pillars; the dining room full of magnificent family portraits; the Dubar Wing with its rich decoration. These splendid rooms are as they were when the royal grandchildren came to stay. You can tour the grounds in a Victorian-style horse-drawn carriage to the Swiss Cottage. Here the children were taught the rudiments of cooking and gardening. The house is open on a daily basis from April to October (Tel: 01983 200022).

## ● Carisbrooke Castle

This is situated just south of Newport and has been in existence for nearly a thousand years. Over that period it has played a prominent part in the critical periods of English history. Perhaps its most famous occupant was Charles I, who was imprisoned there during the Civil War, and who became stuck between the bars of a window when trying to escape. In the castle is housed the Isle of Wight Museum which has a magnificent collection of artefacts belonging to Charles I, Alfred Lord Tennyson and Princess Beatrice. The castle is open daily from April to October (Tel: 01983 522107).

## ● Dodnor Creek Nature Reserve

During the ride you will cycle over a rickety old railway bridge, and this will enable you to have an aerial view of this reserve. Originally the creek flowed directly on to the mudflats of the Medina Estuary, but it was dammed in the 1790s to facilitate a tidal corn mill and a mainly fresh-water pond was formed. It has silted up over the years, enabling a range of vegetation to grow. At very high tides, the salt water from the River Medina floods into the pond, to create a brackish environment and facilitate the growth of a wider range of plant life.

Newport Quay.

**Starting Point:** The Riverway industrial estate in Newport.

**Parking and Toilets:** There is room for a few cars where the cycleway starts.

**Distance:** 3 miles (6 miles there and back).

**Maps:** Ordnance Survey Landranger Sheet 196.

**Hills:** None.

**Surface:** Very good. Most of the ride is surfaced with tarmac and is 9ft wide.

**Safety:** There are no particular hazards on this ride.

**Roads and Road Crossings:** Only minor ones on the actual ride, but to reach the start and end of the ride, at Cowes and Newport, it is necessary to cycle on some fairly busy roads.

**Refreshments:** Plenty of choice in Cowes and Newport. There is a nice complex at Newport Quay.

**Cycle Hire:** Offshore Sports, Shooters Hill, Cowes (Tel: 01983 290514).

**Nearest Tourist Information Centre:** The Arcade, Fountain Quay, Cowes, Isle of Wight PO31 7AR (Tel: 01983 291914).

**Route Instructions:**

1. (0.0 miles): Climb the ramp, pass around the very wide six-bar steel gate and join the cycleway. You can take some interesting little excursions down to the shore on this early part of the ride if you wish.

2. (2.0 miles): Cross a small drive that serves a cement depot.

3. (2.1 miles): Pass over a wooden bridge at Dodnor Creek nature reserve.

4. (2.5 miles): Cross a quiet road.

5. (3.0 miles): The cycleway ends by the roundabout at Riverway industrial estate. Carry straight on over this roundabout to find your way into Newport town centre.

Newport Harbour.

## THE TEST WAY
*(Stonymarsh to Stockbridge)*

*There are no more refreshing places in Hampshire, one might almost say in England, than the green level valleys of the Test and Itchen that wind, alternately widening and narrowing, through the downland country to Southampton Water...*
W. H. Hudson from *Hampshire Days*, published in 1903

The Test Way is a long distance footpath that predominantly follows the River Test and runs from Totton continuing as far north as Inkpen Beacon in Berkshire. Like many chalk streams there are few rights of way along the valley for walkers or cyclists, as the river banks tend to be privately owned and remain the preserve of the rich. It is only recently that this beautiful stretch of the Test has been opened up to the public. The section from Stonymarsh to Stockbridge follows the old Test Valley Railway Line which was built in 1865 and replaced the old canal that ran from Redbridge and Andover. Like many other old railway lines in this book, it was closed in the Beeching era in 1964. This ride is by far the easiest of a series of off-road trails that are promoted by Hampshire County Council and published in a series of excellent

*Top:* Stonymarsh car park.

waterproof leaflets (further information in the 'Routes Described in Local Authority Leaflets' section).

### Background and Places of Interest

● **The River Test**
One of Hampshire's twin rivers which together with its sister the River Itchen drains some of the county's most beautiful countryside and never touches the alien ground of another county. The waters are clear, fast flowing and it is one of the most popular game rivers in the country. There is undoubtedly something special about Hampshire's chalk streams — to sit on the bank watching the clear water glide over the bed of waving water weed, to hear the whirr of a fly fisherman's reel, and beyond the willows the splash of a large trout or some other watery creature.

● **Mottisfont Abbey**
This is now a house that belongs to the National Trust but was originally converted from a medieval monastery. An observation of

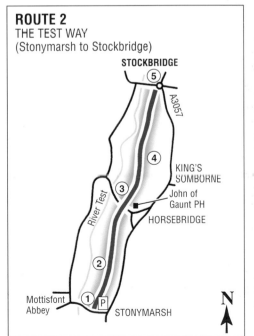

**ROUTE 2**
THE TEST WAY
(Stonymarsh to Stockbridge)

the relative morality of Mottisfont and Stockbridge was made by a Cistercian monk who maintained that he could see devils. He found only one in Stockbridge Fair but found dozens in the priory at Mottisfont. When he caught one and asked about this he was told that souls were easy to come by at Stockbridge, but concentrated effort was required at Mottisfont to provoke even the smallest sin. So expect a perfect place when you visit.

## ● Stockbridge

I prefer country towns to have a High Street of good proportions and Stockbridge is certainly one of these. The street runs from side to side of the narrow valley. Some of the houses in the little town date back to Tudor times and you can find almost every style along the street — timber-framed, brick, plaster — there are no two alike in size or colour. The valley here has provided a river crossing since earliest times, and a posting station existed in Roman occupation. The bridges came later and the

latest one was built in 1962. The name of the town does not come from a crossing place for cattle but means 'log bridge'. Nevertheless, large herds of cattle did cross here at one time and the biggest were from Wales, as they were driven to the great fairs of Surrey and Kent. The coming of the railways put an end to these great cattle drives, but to this day a notice can be seen painted on a former inn at Stockbridge advertising 'Gwair Tymherus, Porfa Flasus, Cwrw Da, a Cwal Cysurus' which means Worthwhile Grass, Pleasant Pasture, Good Beer and Comfortable Shelter.

The town was at one time famed for being a 'rotten borough' where the 70 voters on the electoral roll returned two members of parliament. A vote could be bought for about five guineas but inflation caused the rate to go up to 70 guineas in 1790. Richard Steele of *The Spectator* when he sought re-election was not elected because he reputedly never fulfilled a promise to present an apple stuffed with guineas to the couple who could first produce a child nine months after his election.

**Starting Point:** From the car park at Stonymarsh.

**Parking:** The car park at Stonymarsh is north of Timsbury on the A3057. Be careful if you carry your cycles on the roof of your car or you will end up with a fine mess, as the headroom is restricted as you enter the car park. At the Stockbridge end, parking is possible along the wide High Street.

**Distance:** 5.4 miles (10.8 miles round trip).

The start of the Test Way.                    *Right:* The sun sets over the River Test.

**Maps:** Ordnance Survey Landranger Sheet 185.

**Hills:** None.

**Surface:** A disused railway line that provides a good stone-based gravel track.

**Safety:** There are no particular safety hazards.

**Roads and Road Crossings:** The route crosses one road at Horsebridge.

**Refreshments:** When enjoying the all-too-rare experience of cycling along a river bank, I always take a picnic and I advise you to do the same. But if you have been unable to prepare one there is no shortage of places where refreshments can be obtained. There is plenty of choice in Stockbridge which has many tea rooms and pubs. Also there is the Bear and Ragged Staff at Michelmersh, the John of Gaunt Inn at Horsebridge (half-way along the route) and the Crown Inn at King's Somborne.

**Nearest Tourist Information Centre:** 1 Latimer Street, Romsey, Hampshire SO51 8DF. (Tel: 01794 512987)

**Route Instructions:** Very little directions are necessary as the route is extremely simple and you basically just follow the old railway track:

1. (0.0 miles): From the car park, go north along the disused railway track.

2. (1.0 miles): Continue north along the disused track and join the Test Way.

3. (2.5 miles): Cross the road at Horsebridge, taking care as the traffic can be fast even though it is only occasional.

4. (3.2 miles): You will cross the Clarendon Way here.

5. (5.4 miles): The route finishes at Trafalgar Way in Stockbridge. It is only a short distance to the hospitality of Stockbridge from here. If you would like to make this into a circular route and are able to do a little on-road cycling, take the A30 towards Salisbury ($\frac{1}{2}$ mile and busy) and then turn left on to the quiet back road on the other side of the River Test to return through Houghton and Mottisfont.

**ROUTE 3**
THE NEW FOREST
(A Circular ride around Denny)

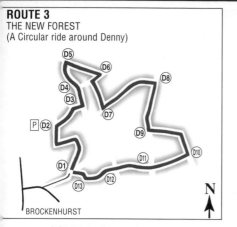

BROCKENHURST

N
↑

## THE NEW FOREST
*(A circular ride around Denny)*

*For never have I known any human habitation,*
*in a land where people are discovered dwelling in so many secret, green, out-of-the-world places, which had so much of nature in and about it...*
W. H. Hudson from *Hampshire Days*, published in 1903

The New Forest has enormous scope for traffic-free cycling, and as such three of the rides in this book are situated in the New Forest. The whole of the Crown lands of the forest amount to 11,000 acres and in 1991 the Forestry Commission introduced a Cycling Code which encourages cyclists to cycle but to stay on the gravelled roads. In the forest there are over 100 miles of these roads. The fact that they are absolutely ideal for traffic-free cycling is to a large degree coincidental, as they were built to enable timber to be removed from the forest and as such are constructed to withstand the weight of large lorries.

**Background and Places of Interest**

● **Brockenhurst**
When W. H. Hudson wrote his classic book about the Hampshire countryside, *Hampshire Days*, he stayed at Roydon Manor a couple of miles south of Brockenhurst, and

his love of the area is encapsulated in the short quotation above. The name Brockenhurst, at one time popularly supposed to mean Badger's Wood, is now thought to be derived from a Saxon named Broca, or simply a broken wooded hill. It is a pleasant enough settlement, best visited out of season when its population is only half of what it is in August. In the graveyard of St Nicholas' church is a World War 1 memorial to over 100 New Zealand soldiers of the Seventh Division who were brought to army hospitals at Balmer Lawn and Tile Barn Hill. There is also a strange memorial to Brusher Mills who was a famous snake-catcher of the area. There is a pub in the town that is named after him.

● **Beaulieu**
King John granted land around this wooded inlet on the Hampshire coast to the Cistercian order in 1204. There the monks built an abbey of stone and its ruinous state is due more to the Dissolution than the ravages of time, as stone was taken for the construction of Hurst Castle. The refectory became the parish church which is why it has a north/south alignment rather than the more normal east/west. At Beaulieu is the National Motor Museum, a comprehensive collection of veteran and vintage cars, motorcycles and other vehicles, including many famous record breakers. It is one of the best motor museums in the world. Nearby is Bucklers Hard where at one time there were plans for a great sea port, but all that materialised was a shipyard. Many of the wooden ships of the navy were built here from the oaks of Beaulieu and the New Forest. Four ships that fought at Trafalgar were built here (*Agamemnon, Illustrious, Swiftsure* and *Euryalus*) with many other men of war that were towed round to Portsmouth by sailors in rowing boats. It is a beautiful unspoilt place now with a double row of 18th century red-brick houses leading down to the bend in the river. There is a maritime museum with an interesting collection of exhibits connected with maritime history, including many fine models, canon and whalers.

*Left:* The start............

**Hills:** There are some short hills on this ride but nothing too demanding.

**Surface:** Excellent and wide gravelled track.

**Safety:** There are no particular hazards associated with this ride, but you should remember that the New Forest is a working forest and all cycle routes could change at short notice. If you come across timber operations on your ride, stop and dismount and do not proceed until the operator has signalled that he is aware of your presence, then walk with your cycle until you are clear of all machinery. It is also perhaps worth mentioning that adders are quite common in the New Forest, although the chances of receiving a bite are extremely remote.

**Roads and Road Crossings:** None.

**Refreshments**: There is plenty of choice of pubs in Brockenhurst at the beginning and end of the ride.

**Cycle Hire:** New Forest Cycle Experience, The Island Shop, Brookley Road, Brockenhurst Hampshire SO42 7RR (Tel: 01590 624204).

**Starting Point:** Standing Hat car park.

**Parking and Toilets:** Standing Hat car park is north east of Brockenhurst. To get there take the Balmer Lawn Road, by the cricket ground, and turn off left where the road bends, to take the drive to the car park.

**Distance**: 8.5 miles.
**Maps:** Ordnance Survey Landranger Sheet 196.

The Lymington River at Brockenhurst.

*Above:* Standing Hat.

**Supplementary Information Available:**
The Forestry Commission can provide a map showing all the routes that are open for cycling. They also provide an excellent set of maps and directions for five waymarked routes in the forest. For details, refer to the 'Forestry Commission Land and National Parks' section. This ride is one of the recommended routes.

**Nearest Tourist Information Centre:**
New Forest Museum and Visitor Centre, Main Car Park, Lyndhurst, Hampshire SO43 7NY. (Tel: 01703 282269).

**Route Instructions:**
The waymarking provided by the Forestry Commission is the best that I have seen. Directions are either provided on gates or at junctions on a post. I have therefore based my directions on the markers that they have provided. As routes may change, if waymarking arrows conflict with these directions, then assume arrows to be correct.

D1 (0.0 miles): Pass through the gate and take the left-most of the two gravelled tracks.

D2 (1.1 miles): Just before D2 waymarker, swing right and then continue on in a similar direction.

D3 (1.6 miles): At the T-junction turn left.

D4 (1.9 miles): Just before the waymarker, swing left and carry straight on as directed.

D5 (2.3 miles): Turn right. The track between this enclosure and the next is part of a medieval trackway from Salisbury to Beaulieu.

D6 (2.8 miles): Just before Gate D6, there is potential for making an error. You need to swing sharp right before you get to the gate. If you find yourself at an information board about harvesting oak in the New Forest, then you have gone wrong and you should turn around. The gate you want will be behind you.

D7 (3.5 miles): Turn hard left, almost doubling back.

D8 (4.4 miles): Take care on the steep track down to Denny Lodge. It is an area of New Forest commoners' smallholdings and pasture.

D9 to D13 (7.9 miles): Just follow the waymarkers.

D1 (8.5 miles): Arrive back at the car park.

# THE NEW FOREST
*(A circular ride around Burley)*

 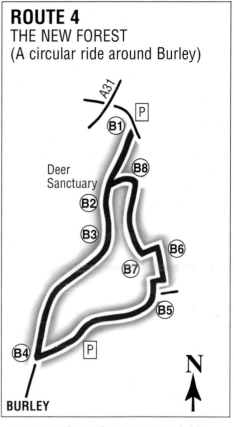

*The tree which moves some to tears
of joy is in the eyes of others only a
green thing that stands in the way.
Some see nature all ridicule and
deformity... and some scarce see
nature at all. But to the eyes of the
man of imagination, nature is
imagination itself.*
William Blake 1798

This is the second of the three rides that are
based in the New Forest. Many parts of the
forest are distinctly lacking in trees which is
often a surprise to the first time visitor, who
might ask the question 'Where is the Forest?' It
is interesting to examine the meaning of the
word 'forest'. To most people there is little
question that it means a wood on a large scale,
but it does not actually mean that at all; it
means a royal property set apart as a sanctuary
for wild animals. If the owner is not the Crown
it becomes a chase rather than a forest. Living
within the boundaries of the forest are
commoners. These are people that have certain
rights that have accrued to them through the
ownership of Forest property. The rights and
the commoners' way of life have existed for
more than nine centuries. There are rights of
pasture where a commoner can graze a
domestic animal in the open forest; the right of
pannage or mast where he is permitted to turn
out his pigs in the autumn so that they can feed
on acorns or beech mast; and fuelwood or
estover which is the right to collect firewood.

## Background and Places of Interest

### ● Lyndhurst
The most relevant reminder of the fact that
Lyndhurst is the administrative centre of the
royal hunting preserve of the New Forest, is
the Tudor Stirrup, which was used by the
authorities for the Norman principle of
expeditation. If a dog was too large to pass
through the stirrup, it was regarded as a risk
to the king's deer and three claws were
removed from each forefoot (expeditated), to

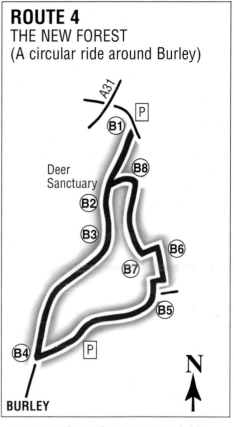

**ROUTE 4**
THE NEW FOREST
(A circular ride around Burley)

prevent poaching. The stirrup is now held in
the Verderers Hall next to the Queen's
House, which is a former hunting lodge and
residence. The management of the forest —
not the growing of timber — has been with
the verderers since the 14th century. The
Forestry Commission was formed in 1919
after the Crown's timber interests had
developed out of proportion with the
commoners' rights. However, there seems to
have been constant friction right up until
1946, but since then the various conflicting
interests of deer management, timber
growing and leisure have been in reasonable
harmony.

*Above:* Perfect waymarking in the New Forest.

*Top:* New Forest Deer Sanctuary.

## ● The Deer Sanctuary

Very soon after you start this ride you will probably see some very fine examples of deer with large antlers, apparently in a field. This will be the deer sanctuary which was started in the winter of 1962. The winter was so bad that the Forestry Commission Keepers started to feed ivy to the deer, and this has been kept up ever since, as ponies naturally feed on ivy when food is scarce in winter. You will see that some trees are pollarded at head height to provide reachable winter feed.

## ● Burley

A village that is very popular with coach tour operators and is probably as typical a New Forest settlement as you can get. There is a legend, (no doubt encouraged by the local tourism association) of the Bisterne Dragon, which was supposed to come down from Burley Beacon for a daily drink of milk. The dragon was probably originally based on an outlaw or wild boar. The name of Dragon Lane still survives in the village.

## ● Canadian Memorial

The Third Canadian Division were camped here in World War 2 and was part of the force assembled for the D-Day Normandy Landings in 1944.

**Starting Point:** At the Canadian Memorial, about 4 miles north of Burley.

**Parking and Toilets:** There is a small car parking area by the memorial. There is a toilet at nearby Bolderwood Car Park.

**Distance:** An 8.9-mile round trip.

**Maps:** Ordnance Survey Landranger Sheet 185.

**Hills:** There are some moderate climbs

**Surface:** Excellent and wide gravelled track.

**Safety:** There are no particular hazards associated with this ride, but you should remember that the New Forest is a working forest and all cycle routes could change at short notice. If you come across timber operations on your ride, stop and dismount and do not proceed until the operator has signalled that he is aware of your presence, then walk with your cycle until you are clear of all machinery. It is also perhaps worth mentioning that adders are quite common in the New Forest, although the chances of receiving a bite are extremely remote.

**Roads and Road Crossings:** Two miles of the 8-mile ride are on a fairly quiet public road.

**Refreshments:** The Queen's Head — a Tudor pub with flagstones, low beams and a good log fire. Likely to be very busy in high summer.

**Cycle Hire:** New Forest Cycle Experience, The Island Shop, Brookley Road, Brockenhurst, Hampshire SO42 7RR (Tel: 01590 624204).

**Supplementary Information Available:** The Forestry Commission can provide a map showing all the routes that are open for cycling. They also provide an excellent set of maps and directions for four waymarked routes in the forest. Contact the Forestry Commission, The Queen's House, Lyndhurst, Hampshire SO43 7NH (Tel: 01703 283141). This ride is one of the four recommended routes.

**Nearest Tourist Information Centre:** New Forest Museum and Visitor Centre,

Main Car Park, Lyndhurst, Hampshire SO43 7NY. (Tel: 01703 282269).

**Route Instructions:**

B1. (0.0 miles): Pass through the barrier to proceed straight on.

B2. (0.8 miles): Continue on at this waymarker avoiding the left turn.

B3. (1.2 miles): Carry straight on here avoiding the right turn. At 2.5 miles you will pass through a barrier, cross a quiet lane, and then pass through a further barrier.

B4. (3.6 miles): Pass through a gate and turn left on to the road. (Take care here.)

B5. (5.6 miles): Where the road bends sharply to the right (by a cottage) turn left off the road.

B6. (6.2 miles): Swing left.

B7. (6.5 miles): Swing right.

B8. (7.6 miles): Proceed straight on and avoid the right turn.

B2. (8.0 miles): Turn right here to return to the start.

B1. (8.9 miles): Back at the start.

*Right:* The Canadian Memorial

## THE NEW FOREST
*(A circular ride around Fritham)*

*But when you have lost your inns
drown your empty selves,
for you will have lost the last of
England.*
Hilaire Belloc

This is the third of the set of three rides that are
based in the New Forest, and this one starts
from Fritham — a village where you will find a
beautiful old and unspoilt country pub. The
ride consists of one mile on Fritham Plain
before entering inclosures, the whole route
being on excellent gravel tracks. The heather
and gorse of Fritham Plain provide a suitable
environment for one of the country's rarest
birds — the Dartford warbler and also the more
common stonechat. The storm of 1990 has
opened up Sloden Inclosure to provide an
opportunity for planting a wider range of
conifers and other broadleaved trees than the
oaks that previously existed there. Depending

on the time of year you will, I am sure, become
very aware of the teeming bird life around you.
You will no doubt see the green woodpecker, a
large green and yellow bird with a crimson
crown. Its flight is readily recognisable with its
dipping nature, but you are even more likely to
experience its loud 'laughing' call which is
known as a yaffle. You may also be blessed by a
glimpse of a kingfisher along Latchmore Brook.
It is always said that if you see a kingfisher, then
you will know it immediately, as its iridescent
blue is unmistakable.

### Background and Places of Interest

#### ● Fritham
Fritham is a quiet little village — one might
possibly say a typical New Forest settlement
of commoners where the people still
exercise their ancient forest rights, putting
their ponies out to graze and their pigs out
for pannage. The village pub (the Royal
Oak) is a particular delight for the enthusiast
who searches out remote country pubs; no
chromium, no music, no fitted carpets, no
hot food, beer in wooden barrels, and a
characterful lady proprietor. When you cross
the threshold it is like stepping into a pub of

*Below:* Fordingbridge, River Avon

30 years ago. There are two basic bars, one with high-backed settles and chairs and pots and kettles hanging in a wide old chimney; there are outside seats and to keep you company outside there will probably be friendly sheep, cows, pigs or ponies wandering nearby.

● **Fordingbridge**

(9 miles west of Fritham)

This is one of the towns that cannot really make up its mind to which county it belongs. It is a picturesque place with its medieval bridge of seven arches which spans the River Avon that has made it such an important crossing point. Its buildings are comparatively young, mostly built in the 19th century due to a large fire that destroyed the old town. The painter Augustus John loved Fordingbridge and did a great deal of work there. Close to the bridge there is a bronze statue erected in his memory. Fairly close to Fordingbridge is an old oak tree that Charles II is reputed to have

hidden in for several days to escape the clutches of the Roundheads. To find the tree turn off for North Gorley on the A338 south of Fordingbridge. The little town is perhaps now best known for being the headquarters of those who come to fish in the River Avon. The Avon cannot compete with the other Hampshire rivers as a trout stream, but has the best coarse fishing the county has to offer

**Starting Point:** This waymarked route starts from Fritham Forestry Commission Car Park.

## ROUTE 5
THE NEW FOREST
(A Circular ride around Fritham)

*Above:* Clearing in the Forest

**Parking and Toilets:** Fritham Car Park.

**Distance:** A 4.4-mile circular route.

**Maps:** Ordnance Survey Landranger Sheet 195.

**Hills:** There are a few short climbs.

**Surface:** Excellent and wide gravelled track.

**Safety:** There are no particular hazards associated with this ride, but you should remember that the New Forest is a working forest and all cycle routes could change at short notice. If you come across timber operations on your ride, stop and dismount and do not proceed until the operator has signalled that he is aware of your presence, then walk with your cycle until you are clear of all machinery. It is also perhaps worth mentioning that adders are quite common in the New Forest, although the chances of receiving a bite are extremely remote.

**Roads and Road Crossings:** None.

**Refreshments:** Although the Royal Oak does not serve hot food, it provides excellent beer and good sandwiches.

**Cycle Hire:** New Forest Cycle Experience, The Island Shop, Brookley Road, Brockenhurst, Hampshire SO42 7RR (Tel: 01590 624204).

**Supplementary Information Available:** The Forestry Commission can provide a map showing all the routes that are open for cycling in the New Forest. They also provide an excellent set of maps and directions for four waymarked routes in the forest. Contact the Forestry Commission, The Queen's House, Lyndhurst, Hampshire SO43 7NH (Tel: 01703 283141). This ride is one of the recommended routes.

**Nearest Tourist Information Centre:** New Forest Museum and Visitor Centre, Main Car Park, Lyndhurst, Hampshire SO43 7NY. (Tel: 01703 282269).

**Route Instructions:** The waymarking provided by the Forestry Commission is the best that I have seen. Directions are either provided on gates or at junctions on a post. I have therefore based my directions on the markers that they have provided. As routes may change, if waymarking arrows conflict with these directions, then assume arrows to be correct.

F1. (0.0 miles): Leave the car park and pass around the barrier into the 'car-free' area. Take the gravelled track that leads you through Fritham Plain towards Sloden Inclosure. At a distance of 0.9 miles by the unreferenced waymarker, bear right.

F2. (1.0 miles): Pass through the gate into Sloden Inclosure.

F3. (1.7 miles): Continue straight on. A little later there is an unreferenced marker bidding you straight on.

F4. (2.1): Pass through the pair of gates to cross the grass driftway. This allows the commoners' ponies free access to other parts of the forest. You also cross the small bridge over Latchmore Brook. A little later there is a non-waymarked junction — bear right here.

F5. (3.1 miles): Turn sharp right after the gate.

F6. (4.4 miles): Pass through the gate to return to the car park.

*Below:* The Royal Oak, Fritham.

**ROUTE 6**
THE MARLBOROUGH TO CHISELDON
RAILWAY PATH

CHISELDON

OGBOURNE
ST GEORGE
Old Crown
Inn

OGBOURNE
ST ANDREW

OGBOURNE
MAIZEY

MARLBOROUGH

N

# THE MARLBOROUGH TO CHISELDON RAILWAY PATH

*A pretty fair town for a street or two — on one side the pent houses supported with pillars which make a fair work*

Samuel Pepys' view of Marlborough in 1668

This is another route made possible by the efforts of Sustrans working in conjunction with volunteers and other national and local organisations. It is constructed on part of the old Midland and South West Junction Railway that ran between Cheltenham and Southampton. The line opened in 1881 and closed in 1961 and was at its peak between the beginning of the century and the start of World War 1. It also carried heavy military traffic during the two world wars.

Work commenced on the path in 1988 and it is now possible to cycle traffic-free from Marlborough to Chiseldon with the exception of a little road-work in Ogbourne St George. It is currently possible to extend the ride to Swindon by the use of minor roads and it is also feasible to utilise the Ridgeway and other tracks to create a demanding, circular and mostly traffic-free route of 16 miles or so. Eventually it is hoped to provide traffic-free links with the Old Town to Toothill Railway Path in Swindon

*Top:* Marlborough Town Hall.

*Above:* The end of the route at Chiseldon.

and with the Kennet and Avon Canal Towpath at Great Bedwyn through Savernake Forest.

I rode this path in July and I have never before seen so many Peacock butterflies. They were feeding on small scabious flowers and there were so many that when I passed and disturbed them, it was like a cloud of dust rising into the air. In fact it was a perfect day to enjoy the experience of riding high above the River Kennet accompanied later by the smooth curves of the Marlborough Downs on either side.

### Background and Places of Interest

### ● Marlborough

The town has always attracted visitors, but suffered a reduction in popularity with the advent of the railway which bypassed it. It has a famous school — Marlborough College — that was originally built as a school for the sons of clergymen and where John Betjeman and William Morris were pupils. It has a very wide High Street with a fine town hall and many Georgian buildings and architectural styles. There are fascinating back alleys to be discovered between the colonnaded shops, with picturesque timber-framed cottages that escaped the great fire of 1653.

### ● Avebury

It only needs a glance at the Ordnance Survey map of the Marlborough area to see that the Marlborough Downs were a centre of population in prehistoric times. Hill forts, burial mounds, strip lynchets occur every few miles and provide a landscape of great antiquity and mysticism. Perhaps the most impressive is the Avebury Stone Circle which is the largest in Europe. Originally consisting of three concentric stone circles surrounded by a massive bank and ditch, it was linked by the West Kennet Avenue of standing stones to the Sanctuary (a temple) at Overton Hill. Hundreds of great sarsen stones from the surrounding downland, often weighing over 20 tons, were used in the construction of the site between 2500 and 2200BC. John Aubrey recommended that King Charles II should visit Avebury as it '…does as much exceed in greatness the renowned Stonehenge as a Cathedral doeth a parish Church…'

### ● Savernake Forest

This is a magnificent expanse of forest consisting of 2,500 acres of unbroken woodland. King Henry VIII hunted deer here and of course married Jane Seymour who was from a local family. Of particular fame is the 4-mile-long Grand Avenue which is accompanied by a nave of beech trees. Edward Hutton perhaps provides us with the most eloquent description of Savernake in his *Highways and Byways in Wiltshire*: 'There is, I think, nothing in southern England quite like Savernake; here is the most ancient home of the greenwood, and there it still finds sanctuary. Far less extensive than the New Forest, it is in comparison with that wild and various region like a jewel to an ocean…'

**Starting Points:**
1. Marlborough. (From the Figgins Lane Car Park the distance is just under a mile to the start and there is a pavement all the way. Turn left [Vauxhall dealer on left] and negotiate the two mini-roundabouts to follow directions to Hungerford [A4]. Immediately after crossing the old railway bridge turn left into Barnfield — the ride starts here.)

2. Chiseldon.

**Parking and Toilets:**
1. Marlborough. (Park in the Figgins Lane Car Park by the River Kennet. There are public toilets and a tourist information office here).
2. Chiseldon. (There is a small car park close to Bush House crossroads, not far from New Farm).

**Distance:** 7.4 miles (14.8-mile round trip).

**Maps:** Ordnance Survey Landranger Sheets 173 and 174.

**Hills**: None.

**Surface:** On the whole very good with a gravel surface. Not quite so good after Ogbourne St George.

**Safety:** Some sections have separated routes for cyclists and horseriders. Keep to the correct section.

**Roads and Road Crossings:** Apart from a couple of minor country lanes which are of little concern, it is necessary to cycle through the village of Ogbourne St George to overcome a missing section of the railway path. However, this is a quiet village as the main traffic is ducted away on the nearby A345.

**Refreshments:** You will be completely spoilt for choice in Marlborough with a riverside coffee house, tea rooms and inns. Ogbourne St George has the Old Crown Inn (18th century free house) which looks very pleasant, and the Parklands Hotel.

**Nearest Tourist Information Centre:**
Car park, George Lane, Marlborough, Wiltshire SN8 1EE. (Tel: 01672 513989).

**Route Instructions:**
1. (0.0 miles): From Barnfield, continue down the unadopted lane for a few yards until you see a wooden barrier on the left. Pass through this to join the railway path and turn right to head north. The route is easy to follow to Ogbourne St George with no directions being necessary until then. You will pass through the occasional gate and barrier.

2. (3.9 miles): The first section of the path ends and you join a quiet road. A few yards further turn left to pass under the main A345. Turn right about 200yd after the Old Crown Inn, and continue until you see Jubbs Lane on the right. Rejoin the path at the end of Jubbs Lane. The route is easy to follow from here to Chiseldon, with one or two obvious minor deviations.

3. (7.4 miles): I terminated the ride at Bush House crossroads as the path from this point onward was not fully suitable for cycling for families.

*Below:* Avebury

# THE KENNET AND AVON TOWPATH

*(Between Pewsey and Devizes)*

*No one, I think, can ever have looked upon this valley enclosed without conceiving a deep affection for it.*
Edward Hutton from *Highways and Byways in Wiltshire* published in 1917

*Above:* Pewsey Station — a picturesque starting point.

This section of the towpath takes us through the beautiful Vale of Pewsey. The landscape could be considered to be of two distinct layers. The first layer consists of the artefacts belonging to the canal. These are present in the form of the bridges, locks, wharves, canalside pubs and other paraphernalia that would not be here were it not for the canal. The second layer is the setting provided by the Vale of Pewsey itself. A pleasant green valley that is the source of the Salisbury Avon and is backed by the escarpment of Salisbury Plain to the south and the slightly unusually shaped Marlborough Downs to the north. Apart from Pewsey Wharf, Honeystreet is the only settlement that is the product of the canal. Its one public house was, at one time, a deeply integrated part of the canalside community. It not only brewed on site but was also a bakehouse and slaughterhouse. This section of the waterway is as reminiscent of a river as a canal as it twists and turns its way around

Stanton St Bernard, Alton Barnes and Allington. Strictly speaking, cycling permits are required for cycling the towpath. These are available free from British Waterways, Devizes (Tel: 01380 722859); Lock Inn Cottage, Bradford on Avon (Tel: 01225 868068); or Avon Valley Cyclery, Bath (Tel: 01225 461880).

## Background and Places of Interest

### ● The Wiltshire Moonraker

Most people know that a Wiltshireman is known as a moonraker. The origin of the legend is claimed by several villages in the area, including nearby All Cannings. Smuggling was common in the 18th century and some villagers had reputedly hidden smuggled brandy kegs in the pond and were using hay rakes to find them. Two excise men appeared and they explained that they were attempting to rake the round cheese (which the excise men saw as the moon's reflection) from the water. Thus the reputation of the poor intellect of the Wiltshireman spread, but the last laugh, of course, was with them.

### ● Pewsey

Pewsey is a quiet downland town that lies about a ¹/₂ mile from the canal. There is a statue of King Alfred in the centre of the town that acts as a reminder that this was at one time part of a Saxon domain. The Pewsey White Horse is one of the best proportioned chalk hill figures in the country and of course there are many. It was prepared in 1937 as a memorial of King George VI's coronation, but it is thought to have replaced an earlier horse that was complete with a rider.

### ● Ladies Bridge and Wilcot Water

Ladies Bridge stands out from the other architecture on this stretch of the canal, with its ornate decoration and balustrades on the parapets. This rather beautiful bridge is no accident but reflects the difficulty that the canal's engineers had in getting permission to pass through the Wilcot Manor estate. Lady Wroughton insisted that the canal would only be allowed to cut through her land if the final product looked like an ornamental lake.

## Starting Point:

A. Pewsey Wharf. (If parking at the railway station it is a ½ mile ride to Pewsey Wharf. Turn left from Station Drive on to the A345, pass under the railway bridge and Pewsey Wharf is on the right.)

B. Devizes, at intersection of canal with A361. If you wish to do the ride from west to east, park in Devizes and follow the A361 for ½ mile and join the towpath at the hump-backed canal bridge (London Road Bridge).

## Parking and Toilets:

A. Pewsey Wharf. There is a small car park at the wharf itself. If full, use the Pewsey railway station car park (pay at ticket desk) or Bouverie Hall car park in Pewsey.

B. In Devizes, there is a car park close to the Corn Exchange which is accessible by Station Road.

There is a toilet at Pewsey Station and also toilets in Devizes.

**Distance:** 11.2 miles (22.4-mile round trip).

**Maps:** Ordnance Survey Landranger Sheet 173.

**Hills:** None.

**Surface:** For the first 10 miles the surface consists of hard-packed earth which when dry is rutted and when wet is rather greasy. The remainder is much better as it is a stone-based path with a gritty top dressing.

**Safety:** Care should be taken when cycling under canal bridges as their curved nature could lead to a nasty blow on the head or shoulder.

**Roads and Road Crossings:** It is necessary to cross the

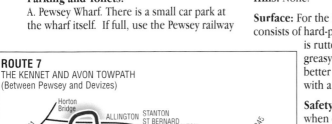

## ROUTE 7
THE KENNET AND AVON TOWPATH
(Between Pewsey and Devizes)

*Above:* Swing-bridge on the Kennet & Avon Canal

occasional road when the towpath changes bank, but these roads are very quiet and there is little hazard.

**Refreshments:** There are eight pubs in Pewsey. The three closest are: the French Horn (canalside at Pewsey Bridge), the Crown and the Royal Oak. Wilcot has the Golden Swan set in pleasant village surroundings. Honeystreet has the Barge Inn — a canalside pub liberally sprinkled with canal lore. All Cannings has the King's Arms and Bishops Cannings the Crown Inn. The Bridge Inn at Horton Bridge is another canalside pub, but looked rather forlorn when I undertook the ride. There is of course plenty of choice in Devizes (see Ride No 12).

**Nearest Tourist Information Centre:** 39 St John's Street, Devizes, Wiltshire SN10 1BL  (Tel: 01380 729408).

**Route Instructions:**

1. (0.0 miles): From Pewsey Wharf follow the towpath under the brick bridge.  Thereafter no directions are needed.  Just follow the towpath signs which consist of a yellow arrow on a white circular background on a green 'finger'.  These will guide you when you need to deviate from the original towpath or when the towpath changes bank.

2. (11.2 miles): The ride ends where the canal meets the A361 in Devizes.

*Below:* Running repairs.

**ROUTE 8**
THE SALISBURY WAY
(Wilton to Fovant)

COMPTON
CHAMBERLAYNE
A30
FOVANT
Salisbury Way
Regimental Badges
BROAD CHALKE
BISHOPSTONE
Queens Head PH
P
Wilton
House
**WILTON**

*Above:* Knapp Down.

## THE SALISBURY WAY

*( Wilton to Fovant)*

*For my own part, I think there is something peculiarly sweet and amusing in the shapely-figured aspect of chalk hills, in preference to those of stone, which are rugged, broken, abrupt and shapeless.*
Gilbert White from *Letter 56.*

When I undertook to write this book, I was initially worried that I would be unable to find a sufficient number of traffic-free rides, but my beloved county of Wiltshire came to my aid in no small way. Wherever you go in the South Wiltshire Downs, the Marlborough Downs or around Salisbury Plain, you will find ancient ridgeways that, by and large, make excellent traffic-free cycling. They are not prescribed cycle routes and can therefore be somewhat demanding, but at most times of the year they are dry due to the chalk subsoil. You will hardly meet a fellow cyclist or walker all day and you will have them to yourself. This route terminates where you meet the road, just above Fovant, although if you are feeling energetic you

can carry on all the way to White Sheet Hill which gives you a round trip of 22 miles of traffic-free cycling.

**Background and Places of Interest**

● **Wilton House**
This is one of England's most beautiful stately homes and is built on the site of a Saxon Abbey. The original house was Tudor and was built on lands given to Sir William Herbert by Henry VIII and this was largely destroyed by fire in 1647. The current house was built in 1653. The grounds are particularly attractive and are enhanced by the chalk stream of the Nadder which flows quietly through. The Palladian Bridge, standing to the south of the house is well known as a very fine example of this type of architecture.

● **The Salisbury Way**
Known by a variety of names, but perhaps this one is the most frequently used, it is one of three Wiltshire ridgeways that run east/west. At Salisbury it climbs Harnham Hill in the east and is without a break until it descends White Sheet Hill above Berwick St John, a distance of some 16 miles. It was a

more direct route than the riverside roads which meander from village to village along the Nadder and Ebble valleys, and because of this it was well used until the arrival of the railways and motor transport. From the Middle Ages until the Dissolution it was probably used by religious pilgrims as a route between Salisbury, Wilton Abbey and Shaftesbury Abbey and when that ceased it was kept in use by travellers on horseback who preferred the easier going of the chalky ridge than the heavier valley routes.

**Starting Point:** From the recommended car park (see below) the starting point is about 1 mile. Proceed along South Street for about ½mile, and take the right turn marked Bulbridge to start the ride by turning left at 'Public Right of Way' opposite a farmyard. This starting point is Point 1 on the map.

**Parking:** Park in the small car park in the square by Wilton Baptist Church. You can park here all day on Sundays but on Mondays to Saturdays it is limited to 2hr. There is an alternative car park nearby in South Street.

**Distance:** 6.5 miles (13-mile round trip).

**Maps:** Ordnance Survey Landranger Sheet 184.

**Hills:** There is only one climb of 120m up to the ridge level.

*Below:* A colourful view from the way.

### ● Fovant Military Badges

These are hill figures cut in the downs above Fovant Village. They are best seen from a distance, for example the A30 trunk road below, but a close-up view can be obtained by walking a few yards from the Salisbury Way. Most of them were originally cut by soldiers stationed locally during World War 1 and contain both British and Australian regiments. They are maintained by various organisations and when I was up there recently a party of scouts were replacing the chalk facing.

**Surface:** The route is an ancient trackway and is therefore unsurfaced for almost all of its length. Being on chalk it is well drained and would usually be expected to be dry from May to September, unless the weather has been very wet. Sections of the route are rutted and the nature of the surface makes it harder work than some of the other rides in this book. Mountain bikes are therefore advisable.

**Safety:** Keep your speed down when descending on a chalk surface to avoid throwing up large flints. Also, the fact that the route is a byway means that it is used by the occasional tractor. You should therefore avoid high speeds as you could get your front wheel stuck in a longitudinal rut with painful consequences.

*Above:* Wilton House.

**Roads and Road Crossings**: None.

**Refreshments:** There are no facilities on the route. If you are taking a picnic, then stop above the military badges at Fovant Down to enjoy a good view. This is reached by a short footpath from the Salisbury Way just before the end of the ride. If you wish to descend from the ridge into the Ebble Valley, then there is the Queen's Head in Broad Chalke. There is of course plenty of choice in Wilton: the Six Bells, the Wheatsheaf, and an attractive coffee shop called D's Delights.

**Nearest Tourist Information Centre.**
Fish Row, Salisbury, Wiltshire SP1 1EJ
(Tel: 01722 334956).

**Route Instructions:**

1. (0.0 miles): Take the 'Public Right of Way' up the hill away from the road.

2. (0.8 miles): When you arrive at the avenue of beech trees, turn right to follow the avenue.

3. (1.2 miles): At a small clearing in the woods, where a byway crosses your route diagonally, keep straight on.

4. (1.5 miles): Join the Salisbury Way (not marked) by turning right. The route initially runs within an avenue of beech trees and then leaves them to run between high hedgerows.

5. (3.9 miles): You meet a slightly more heavily used route on its bend. Join this for about 0.2 miles to continue on in roughly the same direction, until you leave it (as it turns sharply left) by keeping straight on. There is a stile on the right at this point.

6. (6.5 miles): Here you meet the crossing road that takes you steeply downhill for a mile into Fovant. This marks the end of your route. However, if you are feeling energetic you can cycle a further 10 miles (there and back) to White Sheet Hill where the Salisbury Way meets the A30 trunk road. Alternatively if you are happy cycling along country roads then a return along the Ebble Valley, perhaps with a stop at the Queen's Head at Broad Chalke, would be enjoyable.

*Above:* Fly fishing on the River Wylye.

## GROVELY WOOD ROMAN ROAD
*(Wilton to Wylye)*

*... Tis 'Grovely'; an' ael 'Grovely',*
*Thame shouten ael the day*
*To keep thic hankshent custom up*
*On girt Woak Apple Day.*
Old Wiltshire Rhyme sung on Oak Apple Day

This ridge ride takes you along part of the old
Roman road that runs from Sorviodunum (Old
Sarum) to the Mendips. It follows the ridge of
high downland that divides the chalk streams of
the Wylye and the Nadder that are destined to
eventually meet in Wilton. Although it is
classified as a bridleway, it is for the most part
of very sound surface, paying tribute to the
capabilities of the Roman engineers, and
latterly the need to transport timber. The route
is around 600ft above sea level and
consequently there are some good views,
especially of Salisbury Cathedral and Old
Sarum, although for a good part of the ride you
are flanked by avenues of the proud and high
beech trees of Grovely Wood. These provide a
considerable amount of pleasant and airy shade
which makes this a cool and comfortable ride to
do in high summer.

### Background and Places of Interest

● **Grovely Wood**
In the valleys of the Nadder and Wylye below
Grovely Wood lie the villages of Barford St
Martin and Great Wishford. From pre-
Christian times, the villagers have exercised
their right to the wood of Grovely; the
Wishford folk take the greenwood but the
Barford folk only have the dead as they have
sold their right to the lord of their manor for
an annual payment of £5. Both villages make
their claims to this right on Oak Apple Day
(May 29th), when they dance to Salisbury
Cathedral singing 'Grovely! Grovely!! and all
Grovely!!!' and affirm their right before the
High Altar.

● **The Great Wishford Breadstones**
If you return via the Wiltshire Cycleway, look
out for the Breadstones, set in the wall by the
church. These record the price of bread
since 1800 and provide an interesting
snapshot of the cost of living and the impact
of two world wars.

● **The Wilton Carpet Factory**
The factory has been here since 1655 and
received its Royal Charter in 1699 from

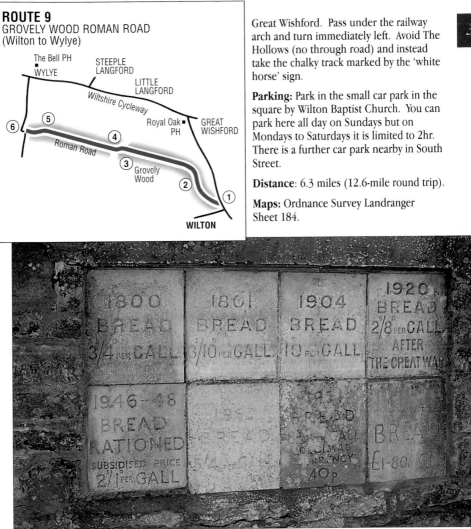

## ROUTE 9
### GROVELY WOOD ROMAN ROAD
(Wilton to Wylye)

The Bell PH
WYLYE

STEEPLE
LANGFORD

LITTLE
LANGFORD

Wiltshire Cycleway

Royal Oak PH    GREAT
WISHFORD

Roman Road

⑥ ⑤ ④

③ Grovely
Wood

② 

① 

**WILTON**

Great Wishford. Pass under the railway arch and turn immediately left. Avoid The Hollows (no through road) and instead take the chalky track marked by the 'white horse' sign.

**Parking:** Park in the small car park in the square by Wilton Baptist Church. You can park here all day on Sundays but on Mondays to Saturdays it is limited to 2hr. There is a further car park nearby in South Street.

**Distance:** 6.3 miles (12.6-mile round trip).

**Maps:** Ordnance Survey Landranger Sheet 184.

*Above:* The Great Wishford Breadstones.

William of Orange. In 1995 it was taken over by an international company who scandalously tried to close it. Thankfully, it has now re-opened, is under sympathetic management and relies on visitors as well as carpet-making to provide income.

**Starting Point:** From the recommended car park (see below) the starting point is about ½mile. Travel along West Street, then turn right by The Bell public house, signposted

**Hills:** One initial climb of about 90m from Wilton to Grovely Hill. Thereafter the route follows the ridge and is basically flat.

**Surface:** Alternates between a stone-based and chalky track, but on the whole is good. A possibility of some wet spots between October and April.

**Safety:** Keep speed down when descending on a chalk way to avoid throwing up large flints.

*39*

**Roads and Road Crossings:** None.

**Refreshments:** When you are on a chalk ridgeway in southern England there is usually a good pub at the foot of the hill every few miles. Here is no exception and if you like old country pubs with character, then I can personally recommend The Bell at Wylye which has the most enormous stone fireplace and also comfortable beds if you wish to stay the night. Also the Royal Oak at Great Wishford does good food and is also alongside the Wiltshire Cycleway. Finally, Wilton offers a good mix of pubs and coffee shops.

**Nearest Tourist Information Centre:**
Fish Row, Salisbury, Wiltshire SP1 1EJ
(Tel: 01722 334956).

**Route Instructions:**
1. (0.0 miles): Take the track up the hill in the direction indicated by a blue arrow on 'white horse' sign.

2. (0.8 miles): By the red brick farm buildings, bear slightly right and leave the avenue of trees, to cycle past the blue Grovely Wood sign, and head straight up the hill on the chalky track, to enter Grovely Wood by passing around the barrier.

3. (3.2 miles): Pass around a second barrier, avoid turning right on the more obvious route, to carry straight on what looks like a footpath.

4. (3.4 miles): You meet a well-surfaced road, turn left on to this, and then swing immediately right, away from the green 'No Through Road' sign. You soon leave the well-surfaced road, to continue on a gritty track very much as before, passing through a wire mesh gate.

5. (5.6 miles): Leave Grovely Wood by passing around a further wire mesh gate. At the asbestos barn, swing left.

6. (6.3 miles): The ride terminates at the Dinton/Wylye road. Here you can retrace the route, or if you do not object to quiet country lanes with the occasional vehicle, you speed down the hill to the road at the bottom and turn right to use the Wiltshire Cycleway to

*Above:* On the old Roman road.

*Above:* Moors Valley Visitor Centre.

# THE CASTLEMAN TRAILWAY
*(Moors Valley Country Park to West Moors)*

This is one of two rides that utilise sections of the old Southampton to Dorchester railway line. The Castleman Trailway is a recreational route that covers part of the old railway and is 16 miles long. Unfortunately it is not possible to cycle traffic-free for the whole stretch and at the moment it is a continuous path for walkers only. The line was originally built to provide a link between Southampton and Dorchester and the route meandered across the New Forest to Ringwood and then via Wimborne Minster to Hamworthy before heading west to Dorchester. The line had the nickname of 'Castleman's Corkscrew' after Charles Castleman, who was a local solicitor responsible for the construction of the line. The other element of the name came from the many twists and turns along its route. The route is generally waymarked by a locomotive superimposed on a footprint.

**Background and Places of Interest**

### ● Moors Valley Country Park
This ride starts from the car park at the country park and the early part of the ride takes advantage of the many permissive cycleways within the park area. The park is a joint venture between Forest Enterprise and East Dorset District Council and it is not surprising that it is one of the most popular attractions in the south of England, as it has something to interest everyone. There are 20 exciting pieces of play equipment for children in the forest, a narrow gauge steam railway, an 18-hole golf course, coarse fishing and as you would expect, acres and acres of freedom for walking and cycling. It is possible to hire cycles from the visitor centre (Tel: 01425 470721 — Warden's Office).

### ● Avon Forest Park
This is a nearby heath and woodland country park near Ringwood, and is run by Dorset County Council. There are picnic sites and car parks for walkers and cyclists and there is a programme of events and guided walks throughout the year.

### ● Ringwood
Once you are off the main road which thankfully bypasses the town, you will find an interesting old town whose market and fairs date from the 13th and 14th centuries and whose breweries were at one time famous for their strong ales, utilising the local river water and barley from the nearby chalk country. There is an interesting link between Ringwood and the subject of our ride — the Castleman Railway. The Lamb Inn was reputedly originally erected to serve as a station on the line, but as the railway construction progressed it was discovered that it had been built a quarter of a mile away from the railway. It was never used as a station and lay neglected for a time until it became the Lamb Inn.

*Below:* The Castleman Trailway.

**ROUTE 10**
THE CASTLEMAN TRAILWAY
(Moors Valley Country Park to West Moors)

Visitor Centre ①
②
③
Hut
④
Moors Valley Country Park ⑩
⑤
⑨
⑥
ASHLEY HEATH
WEST MOORS
⑧
⑦

N

**Starting Point:** Moors Valley Country Park.

**Parking and Toilets:** Use the pay and display car park at the country park. There are toilets in the Visitor Centre.

**Distance:** 7.9 miles total ride.

**Maps:** Ordnance Survey Landranger Sheet 195.

**Hills:** None.

**Surface:** This is excellent; either a gravelled way in the country park area, or a broad stone-based track on a dismantled railway trackbed.

**Safety:** There are no particular hazards to mention.

**Roads and Road Crossings:** There is one road to cross on the outward section at Ashley Heath. This is a small but often busy road, but the authorities have provided a well-designed crossing point. On the return leg, it is necessary to cycle for a short distance along a very quiet residential street, cross the same road as the outward leg and utilise the short drive to the country park.

**Refreshments:** There is a spacious tea room and country shop within the Visitor Centre, which has been built from two timber barns dating back to the 16th century. There is nothing on the route, but there is a nice spot for a picnic by the Moors River which you pass at about 4½ miles (outward) and 6½ miles (inward).

**Nearest Tourist Information Centre:** The Furlong, Ringwood, Hampshire BH24 1AZ (Tel: 01425 470896).

**Route Instructions:**

1. (0.0 miles): At the opposite end of the car park from the Visitor Centre, take the trail marked 'Ashley Trailway Link' in a roughly southeasterly direction.

2. (0.2 miles): Turn left as indicated 'Ashley Trailway Link'.

3. (1.1 miles): Immediately after leaving the horse-free area at a cross-ways, turn right into 'Pine Avenue' (unmarked); you will soon pass a low wooden hut on the right.

4. (1.8 miles): At a five-way junction, turn right to follow the route indicated by a sign 'Horse Trail' and bear right again to follow the white horseshoe signs — there will be two sets of power lines accompanying you on the left.

5. (2.2) miles): Turn left as indicated 'Exit to Ashley Trailway' to cross under power lines and then turn right to join the trailway.

6. (2.9 miles): Pass through the wooden barrier to cross the Ashley Heath to Three Legged Cross road by The Forge newsagents, taking great care.

7. (4.9 miles): At the point where a sign says, 'Trailway ends for riders — Rejoin at Dolmans

Crossing', turn right as directed to 'West Moors ¾mile' to pass through a galvanised steel gate, and then to continue in roughly the same direction through military land with fencing on either side.

8. (5.3 miles): The wooden barriers backed by galvanised steel gates mark the end of this traffic-free section, turn around here and retrace your route. To return you can merely follow your outgoing route, or as an alternative:

9. (7.1 miles): Turn left as directed to 'Moors Valley Country Park ¾mile' to pass through a wooden barrier and follow a quiet residential road.

10. (7.3 miles): Turn left on to a road for a few yards and then turn right into the drive to Moors Valley Country Park and Forest.

1. (7.9 miles): Arrive back at the country park.

*Below:* Ashley Heath station.

# THE CASTLEMAN TRAILWAY
*(Wimborne Minster to Upton Country Park)*

This is the second of two rides that utilise a section of the old Southampton to Dorchester railway line. This ride takes you from a pub on the outskirts of Wimborne (the Willet Arms) to Upton Country Park. The ride follows the old railway line fairly closely, but where the original route is now lost you should follow the waymarkers, even if they lead you away from the old line. The first part of the ride is through a cutting and although there are no views, it is heavily wooded and quite beautiful. The final part of the ride leaves the old railway line and follows an old Roman road to Upton Country Park. The waymarker signs are a green pointer, on which is superimposed a yellow footprint, on which in turn is superimposed a green locomotive. When you reach Upton Country Park, you can extend your ride by an extra mile or so by joining the Holes Bay Cycleway to Hamworthy or Poole.

## Background and Places of Interest

### ● Wimborne Minster

Wimborne is a beautiful old market town situated in the heart of rural Dorset where the Rivers Allen and Stour join. From whichever way you approach the town, you will see the imposing towers of the Minster church of St Cuthburga, which was founded in AD705. It is a fine Norman building with a splendid astronomical clock. You will probably notice references to Quarterjack throughout the town, which is a life-sized soldier which strikes the quarter hours on the side of the West Tower. Entrance to the Minster is free.

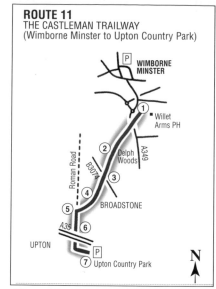

**ROUTE 11**
THE CASTLEMAN TRAILWAY
(Wimborne Minster to Upton Country Park)

If you wish to enjoy a restful hour, there is an interesting model town at one tenth scale, surrounded by attractive gardens which is open every day during the summer months (Tel: 01202 881924). There is also the Priests House Museum which is situated in an old Elizabethan town house and tells the story of the people who have lived and worked there in a series of period rooms and shops. It is also open every day during the summer months (Tel: 01202 882533).

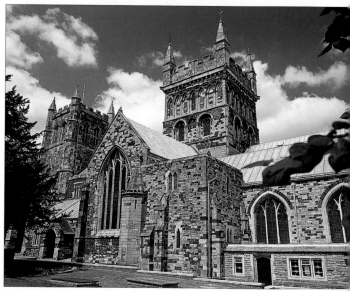

*Above:* The minster church of St Cuthburga.

The memory of Wimborne that stays with me and leads me to think that the founding fathers had Teutonic forebears, is that everything to do with the town seems to be numbered. Not only is each footpath and bridleway numbered, but also the precise number of spaces in each and every car park is also recorded.

### ● Walford Mill Craft Centre

This is housed in a converted water mill, by the river on the north side of the town. On show here is the best of modern craft work from local craftsmen. There are two workshops that are often in use, and a licensed restaurant. The mill is open virtually every day except Mondays between January and March (Tel: 01202 841400).

**Starting Point:** Wimborne is one of those historic old towns whose equilibrium has been completely spoilt by the motor car. You are prevented from cycling where you wish because of intensive one-way systems. To get to the starting point from Park Lane Car Park, follow the nearby street containing the Post Office to its end by the Quarterjack Surgery, and turn left and then sharp right at the roundabout to follow the road that is named Rodway. Whatever you do, avoid following the directions 'all through traffic', as this will take you in a very circuitous long-winded route. You will come to the Willet Arms after about 1 mile.

### ● Upton Country Park

There is a great deal to attract the visitor to this small country park no matter what the season. There is an interesting heritage centre where there are displays of countryside crafts. Outside there is a magnificent walled garden with traditional and modern varieties of roses, camellias and lovely old herbaceous plants. Close by there is a winter garden where varieties such as red dogwood, silver birch and various heathers are chosen for their winter colour. There is also a Romano-British farm portraying agricultural life in the first few centuries AD.

**Parking and Toilets:** As you drive into Wimborne from the south you will find that the town has a good selection of car parks. I parked in Park Lane pay and display car park, which is fairly close to the start of the ride at the Willet Arms. To find this particular car park on arrival, follow signs from the A31/A349 junction for the town centre and turn left for Park Lane. The car park is by The Cricketers pub. If you prefer, you may be able to park in the Willet Arms car park (especially if you are willing to patronise the pub), but you must ask first. There are also car parks at Station Approach Broadstone, Delph Wood and Upton Country Park (which also has toilets).

*Below:* Café at Upton Country Park

**Distance:** 4.1 miles (8.2 miles there and back).

**Maps:** Ordnance Survey Landranger Sheet 195.

**Hills:** Virtually none, the incline of the old line is barely noticeable.

**Surface:** The surface is excellent, and averages about 3yd wide.

**Safety:** There are no particular hazards associated with this ride.

**Roads and Road Crossings:** Most crossings are by underpass, the main exception being the need to cross busy roads at the end of the old Roman road, to gain access to Upton Country Park.

**Refreshments:** There are plenty of places to eat and drink in Wimborne. Among the more attractive looking places are The Cricketers which is immediately by the Park Lane Car Park; The Minster Tea Rooms; the Pudding and Pye. There are also the Heritage Tea Rooms at Upton Country Park. About ½mile into the ride, at Merley, there is rather a good-looking Egon Ronay recommended restaurant.

**Nearest Tourist Information Centre:** 29 High Street, Wimborne Minster, Dorset BH21 1HR (Tel: 01202 886116).

**Route Instructions:**

1. (0.0 miles): Turn left off the road immediately after the Willet Arms car park, you will see a trailway marker board — join the trailway here.

2. (1.3 miles): The route deviates to avoid some houses and climbs a bridge over the drive to the golf club.

3. (1.8 miles): Pass through a couple of underpasses to take you under the B3074 and through a more built-up area (Broadstone).

4. (2.7 miles): The route leaves Broadstone and becomes more rural.

5. (3.1 miles): Descend from the old railway line and on to the old Roman road and turn left.

6. (4.0 miles): Here you will meet civilisation again. You will be carefully routed through an underpass, then join the cycle lane alongside the road, to follow the signs to Upton Country Park.

7. (4.1 miles): Arrive at Upton Country Park.

*Below:* The start of the route at the Willet Arms.

*Above:* Preparing to climb Caen Hill.

## THE KENNET AND AVON TOWPATH

*(Between Devizes and Hilperton)*

*If there is any deader town than Devizes in this country or any other, the present writer has no acquaintance with it.*

William Black, 19th century writer

When I think back to this ride, memories of a very hot July day with a clear blue sky come to mind. Wildlife was abundant with a heron lazily keeping ahead of us by taking short hopping flights, many kestrels were hovering along the banks and processions of swans with their cygnets proceeded past in stately fashion. As it was a Sunday, there was a lot of activity taking place. On the storage ponds by Caen Hill locks there were some colourful games of canoe polo being played and from Seend to Hilperton there were many people engaged in angling, with the most enormous rods, capable of bridging the canal. From time to time these slowed progress as some of the rods were drawn across the towpath, although most anglers were very quick to remove the obstruction. Strictly speaking,

cycling permits are required for cycling the towpath. These are available free from British Waterways, Devizes (Tel: 01380 722859); Lock Inn Cottage, Bradford on Avon (Tel: 01225 868068); or Avon Valley Cyclery, Bath (Tel: 01225 461880).

### Background and Places of Interest

#### ● Devizes

I cannot agree with Willam Black's observation, although to excuse him, he had just experienced the pleasures of Bradford on Avon and Bath. Devizes is the home of Wadworths Brewery and their famous 6X ale and that alone makes it a noteworthy place, although things were not always this way. I spent my youth in various parts of Wiltshire in the days of the dawning of sparkling keg beers like 'Watneys Red Barrel'. The quality of the brewery's bitter did not compare well in those days with the new beers and was often described as 'a pint of old and filthy'. Devizes is a market town with a large market place and many handsome buildings dating from when the wool trade was dominant in these parts. Some local people say that the Bear Hotel has a direct pipeline to the brewery. It sits facing the market place and the cross, where if you have time, you can read about a certain Ruth Pierce who met an untimely death through telling a lie.

## ● Devizes Lock Flight

There are 29 locks on the canal at Devizes and these can be divided into three groups. Seven are at Foxhangers, the famous flight of 16 at Caen Hill and six more between Caen Hill and Devizes town. The completion of the Devizes locks in 1810 marked the end of the canal project that started in 1794 in Bradford on Avon and Newbury. The canal and Caen Hill locks are truly outstanding as they rise up toward Devizes looking like a giant's backbone. Their water storage ponds and beautiful symmetry do more than enough to justify their labelling as 'the most spectacular lock flight in England'.

## ● The Wilts and Berks Canal

At Semington you will find a memorial to this canal that marks its junction with the K&A. If it were not for the information sign that has now been provided, it would be easy to walk past the starting point without noticing it. It was a fairly major achievement in itself, being 51 miles in length. It was completed in 1810 and wended its way via Melksham, Lacock and Swindon to join the Thames at Abingdon. A further canal (the North Wilts) joined Swindon with the Thames and Severn in 1819. As was the usual pattern, it suffered heavily against railway competition, and also in this case an interminable number of locks which led to an end of traffic by 1906.

**ROUTE 12**
THE KENNET AND AVON TOWPATH
(Between Devizes and Hilperton)

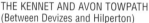

*Above:* Wildlife abounds on the canal.

**Starting Point:**
A. At London Road Bridge, Devizes (intersection of canal with A361). From the Corn Exchange Car Park, follow the A361 east for ½mile and join the gravelled towpath by descending the steep slope on the left of the road on the southwest side of the bridge.
B. Alternatively, the Visitor Centre at Devizes Wharf. If starting at the wharf, use the car park situated there.
C. Alternatively, Hilperton Marina.

**Parking and Toilets:**
A. I used the car park close to Devizes Corn Exchange which is accessible by using Station Road.
B. The Visitor Centre at Devizes Wharf (Pay and Display).
C. Hilperton Marina has extensive car parking and toilets.

**Distance:** 10 miles (20-mile round trip).

**Maps:** Ordnance Survey Landranger Sheet 173.

**Hills:** On your return to Devizes, you will undertake a gentle climb of 234ft in 2½ miles, which is how hills should be.

**Surface:** Excellent, thanks to Sustrans — a stone-based towpath with a gritty top dressing that is quite wide in places and always more than adequate.

**Safety:** Care should be taken when cycling under canal bridges as their curved nature could lead to a nasty blow on the head or shoulder.

**Roads and Road Crossings:** There is one where you need to be careful and that is where you cross the A361 again, by Caen Hill locks.

**Refreshments:** There is plenty of choice in Devizes from the famous Bear Hotel through to coffee shops and many pubs. The Black Horse close to the lock flight in Devizes provides a pleasant canalside stop and there is also the Artichoke 200yd west of Devizes Town Bridge. Another canalside stop, that I can confirm is very pleasant — as I took advantage of it — is the Barge Inn at Seend Cleeve. Refurbished within the last few years I would say, but still with a

pleasant feeling of the old world about it. At the far point of the ride, along the canalside at Hilperton Marsh there is the King's Arms, a modernised inn and eating place. There are also other facilities at Hilperton Marina where you can buy goods.

**Nearest Tourist Information Centre:**
39 St John's Street, Devizes, Wiltshire SN10 1BL (Tel: 01380 729408).

**Route Instructions:**

1. (0.0 miles): Join the canal at London Road Bridge. There is no need for directions. Just follow the towpath signs which consist of a yellow arrow on a white circular background on a green 'finger'. These will guide you when you need to deviate from the original towpath or when the towpath changes bank. At Devizes you can link with Route No 7 to Pewsey.

2. (10 miles): Hilperton Marina where you end your ride, but you could carry on to Bradford on Avon and link up with Route No 15 to Bath.

*Right:* Devizes Corn Exchange.

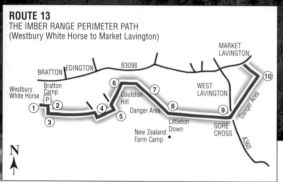

**ROUTE 13**
THE IMBER RANGE PERIMETER PATH
(Westbury White Horse to Market Lavington)

*Above:* Westbury White Horse

# THE IMBER RANGE PERIMETER PATH

*(Westbury White Horse to Market Lavington)*

*Their very emptiness and desolation, which frightens the stranger from them, only serves to make them more fascinating to those who are intimate with and have learned to love them.*

W. H. Hudson referring to the Wiltshire Downs from *A Shepherd's Life,* published in 1910

This ride is one of the most unusual in this book and is a real gem. For the most part the route follows the Imber Range Perimeter Path which skirts a large military training area, and is mainly a ridge route that follows the edge of Salisbury Plain. If the military are not firing,

you will be guaranteed peace and tranquillity with only a lapwing — or in summer perhaps a skylark — to disturb you, but if they are, you will occasionally be made to jump out of your skin. Once you have left the busy area where the public visit Bratton Camp and the white horse, you will be unlucky if you meet anyone. The route followed from Coulston Hill to Littledown is part of the old Salisbury to Bath coach road and you will be reminded of this by the occasional old and virtually illegible milestone.

## Background and Places of Interest

### ● Salisbury Plain

This is odd country — odd but beautiful. Geologically speaking, the plain is a large expanse of elevated chalkland. It is rarely flat as the word 'plain' implies but is gently undulating, and around the edge — or escarpment as it is known — occurs some of the most attractive chalk downland in England. These hills are equal in beauty to

the South Downs, but they have the advantage of almost total solitude which sets them apart from their more southerly sisters. Another feature of the plain is its largely unploughed, uncultivated and ungrazed nature.

I have spent many summer days there and from afar, at that time of year, you could be forgiven for thinking that you were looking at a desert, as the grass grows long and turns yellow, colouring the land for as far as the eye can see.

● **Imber**

It is almost certain that you will never have visited the charming little village of Imber, as few people have seen it since 1943 when it was taken over by the army as part of the Salisbury Plain military training area. It has always been one of the most isolated villages of Southern England. You will not

approach within 4 miles of it on this ride, and due to the lie of the land, you will not see it either. The roads to Imber are occasionally opened to the public on Bank Holidays.

● **Westbury White Horse and Bratton Camp (Iron Age Hillfort)**

At the start of the ride there is, cut into the chalk escarpment of the down above Bratton, the figure of a white horse. There are five similar horses in Wiltshire and this is the only one to have any possible claim to antiquity. In fact the only white horse to be genuinely and undoubtedly ancient is the one at Uffington in Oxfordshire. The present horse was entirely re-cut in the turf by a Mr Gee and was again restored in 1853. The earliest mention of a horse on this site is in a pamphlet of 1742 where it was described as being situated close to a Saxon victory and therefore being comparable to the Uffington white horse.

There is a legend that says that it was cut by the Saxons to commemorate Alfred's victory over the Danes in May 878 at Ethandune (which is generally thought to be Edington). Exactly where this great battle occurred is not agreed. There are two possible sites, one at Bratton Camp, and the other at nearby Edington Hill.

**Starting Point:** This ride starts from Westbury White Horse. Access from the little country town of Westbury is via the B3098 and the directions to the White Horse are well signposted.

**Parking:** Park in the car park intended for visitors to the White Horse and Bratton Castle.

**Distance:** 10 miles (20 miles there and back) if you ride the full distance to Market Lavington. For families with young children, or the less fit, a ride to New Zealand Farm (13 miles there and back) eliminates the worst hill.

**Maps:** Ordnance Survey Landranger Sheet 184.

**Hills:** This is an undulating ride with some stiff climbs.

**Surface:** Good and well drained throughout. Some of the route is surfaced with tarmac (often pot-holed) and some is a chalk and flint track. The nature of the surface makes the use of a mountain bike advisable.

*Right:* The range is well marked.

*Left:* The escarpment of the plain.

**Safety:** You should keep your speed down when descending on a chalk surface to avoid throwing up large flints. Also beware of large pot-holes on surfaced sections. Most of this route is over BOATs, which are byways open to all traffic, and some over minor country lanes which, because they lead to nowhere of importance, are virtually traffic-free. However, you may encounter the occasional tractor or car. From the military viewpoint, you will be perfectly safe as long as you follow the directions and do not stray on to the military training area. Please do not forget that although there may appear to be no military activity, there may very well be unexploded missiles or mines lurking on the range.

**Roads and Road Crossings:** One busy road is crossed — the A360 Salisbury to Devizes road.

**Refreshments:** Do not expect to find a wayside pub on this deserted part of Salisbury Plain, and my recommendation is to take a picnic. There are three pubs in Market Lavington, although at the time of writing none of them looks particularly inviting from a family point of view. There are some nice pubs at the foot of the downs, but these are not on the actual ride. One that I have tried is The Duke at Bratton which is very good, and Edington also offers good hospitality.

**Nearest Tourist Information Centre:**
The Library, Edward Street, Westbury, Wiltshire BA13 3BD (Tel: 01373 827158).

**Route Instructions:**
This is a hilly ride of 20 miles there and back, and could be quite strenuous for the less fit. If you feel like keeping the ride to a more

comfortable distance, I suggest that you take some food and drink - this is essential anyway as you will be in remote country with no wayside places to stop — and picnic on the edge of the track on Littleton Down just after New Zealand Farm — which is a good high finishing point.

1. (0.0 miles): Leave the car park and turn right on the narrow road that runs behind Bratton Castle.

2. (0.1 miles): At the three-way junction, avoid the turning to the left that will take you downhill into Bratton and turn right toward the farm building in the trees. The tarmac surface ends here and the route becomes a wide stony track.

3. (0.2 miles): Turn left to keep the farm buildings previously mentioned on your left.

4. (2.1 miles): Turn sharp right as directed by the perimeter path signs and then when you are by the range checkpoint, turn left.

5. (2.9 miles): Swing sharp left and then right to rejoin a narrow tarmac-surfaced road that is signposted Tinhead Farm, (but do not take the right turn to Tinhead Farm a few hundred yards later).

6. (4.1 miles): At T-junction take right arm of T to rejoin the perimeter path.

7. (5.0 miles): Immediately after the trig point avoid the turning to Stokehill Farm and keep straight on.

8. (6.3 miles): When close to New Zealand Farm Camp, bear half-left if you wish to continue your journey downhill to Gore Cross, and then to Market Lavington. This is a surfaced road with no traffic, but beware of large pot-holes.

9. (8.5 miles): At the collection of farm buildings and bungalows marking Gore Cross, bear left, then cross the main road and take the narrow road that climbs the hill (accompanied by old farm buildings, old tyres, old trailers and pig farms).

10. (10.1 miles): Turn left away from the checkpoint to descend the steep hill to Market Lavington and emerge from White Street.

# THE FOSSE WAY
*(North east from Sherston)*

*'Fight well Rattlebone*
*Thou shalt have Sherstone.'*
*'What shall I with Sherstone doe*
*Without I have all belongs thereto?'*

This ride is along one of the main Roman
military roads and provides you with the
interest of travelling a route that has now
almost fallen out of use and yet at one time was
an important route used by the mighty legions
of the Roman empire. It is therefore an
extremely peaceful ride and I only met two
walkers over the whole route. It could be quite
demanding for young children or the less fit,
not because of hills but because of a surface
that is in many places rough and rutted; but the
Fosse Way has a pleasant habit of treating you
to a well-surfaced section every time you think
that the going is becoming too difficult.
However, as it is a linear route you will have
the advantage of always being able to compare
how tired you are with a precise knowledge of
the remaining journey you still have to
complete.

## Background and Places of Interest

### ● Sherston
A lovely old south Cotswold town,
commanding a high point of land and close to
the source of the River Avon. The town has
two memorials to an early Wiltshire hero —
John Rattlebone. A local inn is named after
him and a little carved figure at the church is
said to be his likeness. He is supposed to have
been involved in a great battle between the
Saxons and Danes in 1016. Ancient records
give 'Sceorstan' as the site of the battle and this

is thought to be Sherston. The story has it
that it was an inconclusive but bloody
battle and Rattlebone received a terrible wound
in the stomach. His bowels began spilling out,
but seizing a tile he held this against the wound
to keep himself intact while fighting on.
Apparently he survived and was given the
manor of Sherston for his bravery and this is
recorded in the old village song that is
recorded at the beginning of this chapter.

### ● The Fosse Way
It ran from Axmouth (via Ilchester, Bath,
Cirencester and Leicester) to Lincoln and the
line is detectable for the most part to this day.
In some places it has been adapted and forms
the basis of modern trunk roads such as the
A37, A429 and A46 and yet in others it is a quiet
unsurfaced byway. The name is derived from
the Latin 'fossa' meaning ditch and this is
thought to have referred to the prominent
ditch or ditches associated with the way. It is
possible that the ditch or ditches were
defensive and the Fosse Way may have defined
a frontier protected by forts. This particular
section of the Fosse Way still forms the county
boundary between Wiltshire and
Gloucestershire.

### ● Badminton
The village, country house and estate that is the
seat of the Duke of Beaufort. The game of
Badminton derives its name from Badminton
House as it originated here in the late 19th
century. It is of course also well known for its
horse trials and hunting history. The village is
attractive, has an unusual feudal atmosphere,
and is worth a visit.

*Below:* Badminton village.

*Above:* Sherston.

**Starting Point:** The starting point is 2 miles from the centre of Sherston at a crossroads where the Fosse Way becomes unsurfaced. (Map reference ST872843). Follow the B4040 east towards Malmesbury to pass Sherston church. Turn right after 0.3 miles (signposted Hullavington 4, Chippenham 11). Bear left at junction (signposted Hullavington 3¾, Chippenham 10). At next junction you will see a left turn marked 'By-way' — this is the starting point of the ride.

**Parking and Toilets:** It is recommended that you park in Sherston. This has a very wide main street which provides plenty of room for parking, but please respect the needs of local folk.

**Distance:** 4.9 miles (9.8-mile round trip). It is possible to extend the distance to 17.8 miles if you are feeling energetic.

**Maps:** Ordnance Survey Landranger Sheet 173.5

**Hills:** None.

**Surface:** The first ½ mile has what might be described as a rubble surface. Thereafter the surface is variable and in many places is unsurfaced and rough. In places it appears that the route is inclined to be wet between October and April and during rainy periods.

**Safety:** It is suggested that you ride steadily as there are several sections where the going is uneven.

**Roads and Road Crossings:** The route follows an isolated rural lane for a short section and crosses two roads. One is a quiet country road and the other is the B4040 where the visibility is not that good.

**Refreshments:** There are none along the route. There is a delightful picnic spot where the ride crosses the River Avon. There are at least two pubs in Sherston — the Rattlebone Inn and the Carpenters Arms.

**Nearest Tourist Information Centre:** Town Hall, Market Lane, Malmesbury, Wiltshire (Tel: 01666 823748).

**Route Instructions:**

1. (0.0 miles): Join the Fosse Way by following the 'By-way' sign. I rode the route during July and was blessed with a magnificent display of blue flowers which a couple of walkers informed me was the chicory plant.

2. (1.0 miles): The Fosse Way continues along a quiet surfaced lane.

3. (1.2 miles): Avoid a very wet section of the way by ignoring the 'By-way' sign which indicates the continuation of the way and instead continue to the crossroads.

4. (1.3 miles): At the crossroads turn right as directed to Malmesbury and Foxley.

5. (1.4 miles): Turn left to rejoin the Fosse Way at the 'By-way' sign.

6. (2.0 miles): Pass through a gate to swing right down the hill to cross the River Avon by a beautiful old stone bridge. Climb the other side of the valley and pass through a wide six-bar metal gate and then a further gate to join a short tarmac stretch until you meet the B4040.

7. (2.6 miles): Cross the B4040 and continue onward.

8. (3.4 miles): Cross straight over the Shipton Moyne/Malmesbury road.

9. (4.2 miles): Cross the small river.

10. (4.9 miles): Here we meet the B4014 Tetbury to Malmesbury road which marks the end of our ride. If you are particularly energetic, it is possible to continue for a further 3½ miles to Kemble airfield, where unfortunately the route has been extinguished.

**ROUTE 14**
THE FOSSE WAY
(Northeast from Sherston)

Merchants Farm

SHIPTON MOYNE

B4040

SHERSTON

River Avon

N

*Above:* The Fosse Way crosses the River Avon.

# THE KENNET AND AVON CANAL TOWPATH
*(Between Bath and Bradford on Avon)*

*The ten miles before Bath was perhaps the worst of all, but the scenery was as beautiful as any that I have ever seen.*
Montague and Ann Lloyd from *Through England's Waterways*

I rode this route in late May and it was one of the most stress-free days that I have ever had. The canal shares the Avon Valley with the river, railway and roads, and you are constantly reminded of how lucky you are having the peace and quiet of the towpath to yourself. Only the 'putt-putt' of the occasional passing boat and the need to wave to the crew will waken you from your musing on the delights of the day. The surface is excellent, thanks to Sustrans, and there is plenty of interest along the way.

## Background and Places of Interest

### ● Bath
Without doubt, one of England's most elegant cities, it is our only source of hot springs. It was not always as elegant, however. In my youth (30-odd years ago), the buildings were horribly blackened by pollution, but since then most have been cleaned up and look wonderful, and there is so much to see and do in Bath.

### ● Kennet and Avon Canal
The canal was finished in 1810 and connected Bristol and Reading. Amongst the most striking features of the canal are the two aqueducts (Avoncliff and Dundas) which you will pass on your ride. Designed by John Rennie, they are dramatically set across the Avon Valley. Strictly speaking, cycling permits are required for cycling the towpath. These are available free from British Waterways, Devizes (Tel: 01380 722859); Lock Inn Cottage, Bradford on Avon (Tel: 01225 868068), or Avon Valley Cyclery, Bath (Tel: 01225 461880).

### ● Claverton Pumping Station
Along the route you will notice water gushing into the canal from the bank. Considering that the canal is many feet higher than the river this compels an investigation which reveals the existence of this amazing piece of engineering. The station is open to visitors every Sunday and Bank Holiday during the summer months. Every time a boat passes through the flight of locks at Widcombe, thousands of gallons of water are lost into the Avon. Engineer John Rennie sited the station here in 1810 to help counteract this, and it is capable of raising up to 100,000 gallons an

hour up to a height of 14 metres from the River Avon. It is driven by a water-wheel powered by the river itself.

### ● Bradford on Avon Tithe Barn

This is situated in Barton Farm Country Park and is a most imposing structure, being 168ft long with a roof supporting over 100 tons of stone tiles. It was built in the mid-14th century to store the tithe, which was one tenth of the produce from the farm, and consisted mainly of hay, corn and wool. The farm was the Abbey of Shaftesbury's home farm (Barton Farm).

*Below:* Kennet & Avon Canal — Sydney Gardens footbridge.

**Starting Point:** Widcombe Locks in Bath

**Parking and Toilets:** There is a car park ideally situated by Bath Cricket Club in North Parade Road. It is only a few yards and a flight of steps to the canal, although it is a little pricey. Just walk to the end of North Parade Road and you will see the blue Kennet and Avon Canal sign that seemingly directs you through a hole in a wall. There are also toilets adjacent to the car park. Bath is a very congested city and it is suggested that you arrive early to avoid traffic problems and

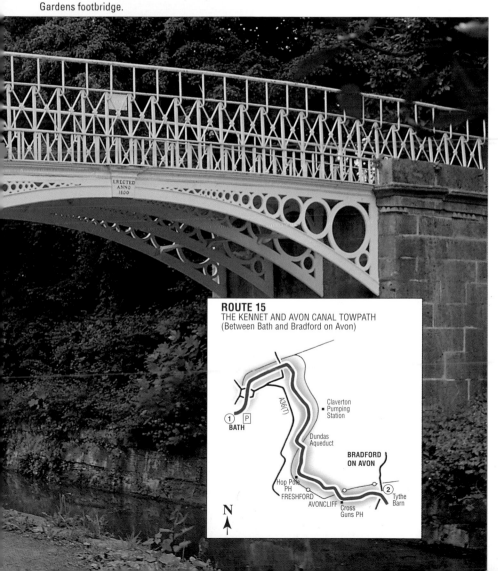

**ROUTE 15**
THE KENNET AND AVON CANAL TOWPATH
(Between Bath and Bradford on Avon)

ensure you can park easily. There is also a car park and toilets near the tithe barn at Bradford on Avon.

**Distance:** 8½ miles from Widcombe Locks to the tithe barn at Bradford on Avon (17 miles total ride).

**Maps:** Ordnance Survey Landranger Sheets 172 and 173.

**Hills:** None.

**Surface:** This is excellent thanks to Sustrans — a broad, stone-based canal towpath with gritty top dressing.

**Safety:** Care should be taken when cycling under bridges as their curved nature could lead to a nasty blow on the head or shoulder.

**Refreshments:** The Hop Pole Inn at Limpley Stoke is ideally placed for a half-way stop. There are signs to direct you and the distance is about 400yd.from the canal. It is a friendly pub with a jovial landlord and good food and ale. The Cross Guns at Avoncliff also looks good and there is the occasional tea/coffee shop promised by small hand-painted signs along the way. Bradford on Avon has plenty to offer as well.

*Below:* The tithe barn, Bradford on Avon.

**Nearest Tourist Information Centre:**
The Colonnades, 11-13 Bath Street, Bath BA1 1SW (Tel: 01225 462831).

**Route Instructions:**

1. (0.0 miles): After climbing the steps, turn left to proceed to Bradford on Avon. Basically all you need to do is to keep a careful eye on the towpath directions which are signified by a yellow arrow. These will guide you when you need to deviate from the original towpath or when the towpath changes bank.

2. (8.5 miles): A suitable place to terminate the ride is the tithe barn at Bradford on Avon, although there is plenty of scope for going further — see the 'Where to Cycle' section of this book.

*Below:* Colourful longboats at Bathampton.

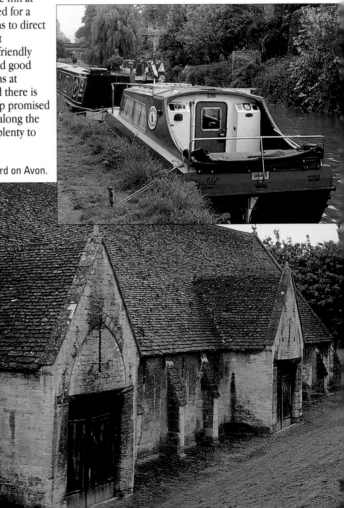

*Left:* Warehouses alongside the Avon.

# THE BRISTOL AND BATH RAILWAY PATH

This route runs for most of its length along the old trackbed of the Midland Railway. It links Bath and Bristol via Mangotsfield. At the Bath end, the first mile along the Avon Towpath is delightful and passes under some attractive bridges. Here, you get a completely changed view of that elegant Georgian city from the busy consumer-driven world that is modern Bath. The railway path was started by Cyclebag which is a Bristol-based cycle pressure group and the final section into Bristol was built by Sustrans between 1979 and 1985. Although in places it is very much a route for people to get to work or do their shopping, some very imaginative ideas have been incorporated into the project. For instance, you will from time to time see sculptures along the way and these give the ride a special quality. Some of them also double as seats or drinking fountains. The trail was the idea of Sustrans and was provided by support and sponsorship from various local organisations.

If you undertake the whole route, it is about 14 miles long. The Bristol end of the route inevitably has a city commuter feel about it, so I cycled from Bath as far as Warmley where the A420 is crossed via a pelican crossing.

## Background and Places of Interest

### ● Bath - The Roman Baths Museum

If you are a visitor to Bath, you must go to the Roman baths. The hot springs are the only ones in Britain, and every single day a quarter of a million gallons of water gush out of the earth at exactly 46.5° C. It is alleged that it was Bladud, legendary father of King Lear who first discovered the springs around 500BC. But it was not until the Romans occupied the area that Bath began to become a place of importance and it was where they built one of the finest temples in Britain dedicated to their goddess Minerva. The hot springs were developed as a sophisticated series of baths which were used for bathing and health purposes. The gilded head of Minerva was discovered in the 18th century, but amazingly, the discovery of the Baths did not begin until 1878, and since then some of the most fascinating Roman remains have gradually been excavated. By the 18th century the city had recaptured the splendour that it had enjoyed under the Romans, and it was transformed from a treatment place of the sick to a centre of fashionable life. The West Bath has recently been extended to display for the first time a Roman swimming pool.

### ● The Avon Valley Railway

This is based at Bitton Station and a holiday service of standard gauge steam trains is provided over a short length of track which looks as if it is currently being extended. At the station there is a large selection of old locomotives and rolling stock that have been saved from the breakers.

### ● Warmley Gardens and Grotto

The main entrance to the gardens is only about 550yd from the railway path and they lie on the site of a factory known as William Champion's Brassworks which occupied the area from 1746 to 1768. It was here, in this factory, that the commercial production of zinc was started. The grottos are an odd collection of chambers which are made of clinker and mortar and it is believed that these are on the site of the very earliest brassworks. The enormous statue of Trident has been recently restored, although it is still missing one prong.

## ROUTE 16
### THE BRISTOL AND BATH RAILWAY PATH

WARMLEY

④

OLDLAND

River Avon

Bird in
Hand PH

SALTFORD

③
②
P
BATH

①

N
↑

**Starting Point:** I started at the Bath end of the railway path from Green Park Road. Being a suburban route, there are very frequent access points at intervals all along the way that are too numerous to mention.

**Parking and Toilets:** I parked in Avon Street Car Park which is very convenient for the start of the railway path at Green Park Road, and enables you to maximise your distance travelled on the route. Another car park that I have used is in Charlotte Street.

**Distance:** My intention was to cycle from Green Park Road in Bath as far as Warmley which is a distance of 9 miles (18 miles there and back) which was a comfortable morning's cycling. The total route is 14 miles long (28 miles there and back).

**Maps:** Ordnance Survey Landranger Sheet 172.

**Hills:** None.

**Surface:** Excellent, much of the route has a tarmac surface.

**Safety:** There are no particular safety hazards.

**Roads and Road Crossings:** There is the occasional crossing of quiet suburban roads. The one serious crossing (of the A420) at Warmley is controlled by lights.

**Refreshments:** The Dolphin Inn is immediately alongside the river path at the Bath end. I stopped at the Bird in Hand at Saltford which is a few yards from the route and is a regular haunt of cyclists. From the garden, you have a good view of the elevated railway path and the cyclists wending their way back and forth. There are also refreshment possibilities at Bitton Station at weekends.

*Above:* The Avon Valley Railway.

**Cycle Hire:** Mud Dock Cycleworks, 40 The Grove, Bristol BS1 4RB (Tel: 0117 929 2151), or Avon Valley Cyclery, Arch 37 (at the rear of Bath Spa Station), Bath BA1 1SX (Tel: 01225 461880).

**Nearest Tourist Information Centre;**
The Colonnades, Bath Street, Bath BA1 1SW (Tel: 01225 462831)

**Route Instructions:**
The route is extremely simple.

1. (0.0 miles): Descend the slope to join the riverside path. The first part of the route is shared with the Avon Walkway.

2. (1.8 miles): The route shares its course with a road for a short distance by the Maltings Industrial Estate.

3. (2.1 miles): Leave the road and industrial area and turn left to join the railway path proper.

4. (8.7 miles): Warmley pelican crossing marks the end of the ride, but a further 5 miles will take you into the centre of Bristol.

*Below:* Tranquillity on the Avon.

# ON THE HILLS AROUND DORCHESTER
*(A high-level ride from Blackdown Hill)*

This ride takes you along the inland version of the South West Coast Path and traverses the ridge of the downs to the south west of Dorchester, from where there are the most marvellous views of Portland, Weymouth and Chesil Beach. It is a linear route and runs due east from the Hardy Monument near Portesham. Conveniently, at the foot of the downs, there is a beautifully quiet little road that can be used for the return leg, thereby converting the ride to a circular one if you have no objections to a little quiet on-road cycling.

## Background and Places of Interest

### ● The Hardy Monument

This part of Dorset is famous for people with the surname 'Hardy'. Dorchester is, of course, the home of Thomas Hardy, the great novelist. It is therefore surprising to find that the Hardy Monument, from where the ride starts, is nothing at all to do with the writer. It is in fact a memorial to Thomas Masterman Hardy who was given command of Nelson's flagship HMS *Victory* in 1803 and led the ship when Nelson was struck down. Nelson is of course supposed to have cried 'Kiss me Hardy' as he lay in Hardy's arms. After Nelson died, he brought the body home and took part in the grand funeral. Afterwards he became First Sea Lord and the Governor of Greenwich Hospital where he died in 1839. The monument was publicly funded in 1844 and has a spiral staircase with 120 steps that take you up 70ft to the top. It commands fine views of the countryside loved by Hardy in his boyhood and a wide stretch of the sea where he passed so much of his life. Unfortunately, it was closed for refurbishment when I cycled the route in 1995 so I was denied the enjoyment of the view from the top of the monument.

*Right:* Thomas Hardy's statue, Dorchester.

### ● Dorchester

There are three 'Hardys' that have connections with Dorset; the naval one mentioned above; a local benefactor who founded the grammar school and whose name you will see around the town, in the Hardye Arcade for example; and Thomas Hardy the poet and novelist. The cottage where Thomas Hardy the writer was born in 1840 is at Higher Bockhampton, a little way out of Dorchester. It was built by his grandfather and is now owned by the National Trust. His other dwelling place in the Dorchester area was at Max Gate, on the Wareham road. This was designed by Hardy, who was also of course a trained architect, and was built by his brother Henry in 1885. He lived at Max Gate with his wife Emma Gifford who died in 1912. He subsequently married Florence Dugdale who went on to outlive him. Hardy used the ancient Saxon

kingdom of Wessex as a background for his novels and used real places but gave them a new identity. For example, his Casterbridge is our Dorchester; and Budmouth Regis is our Weymouth.

Continuing the literary theme for a moment, Dorchester is also the town where the great English dialect poet William Barnes spent most of his working life. He was a schoolmaster by profession and worked at a boarding school in the town. To a certain extent, he was a mentor of Thomas Hardy and he is held in great affection by the town.

There are so many other interesting things to discover in Dorchester: Roman Dorchester, Judge Jeffreys' Bloody Assize, a Military Museum, Dinosaur Museum and the Tutankhamun Exhibition and yet another author — Sir Frederick Treves who wrote the *Elephant Man.*

### ● The Tolpuddle Martyrs

The nearby village of Tolpuddle was the home of six agricultural labourers who were arrested on 24 February 1834 for forming a trade union. They were sentenced to seven years' transportation and were transported to Australia in that same year. There is a museum at Tolpuddle that tells their story (Tel: 01305 848237).

**Starting Point:** The car park at the Hardy Monument.

**Parking:** Park at the car park at the Hardy Monument on Blackdown Hill near Portesham.

**Distance:** 3.4 miles (6.8 miles there and back) that are traffic-free. Alternatively a circular route can be created if the option of using the quiet country road at the foot of the downs is taken for the return leg, and this gives a total ride of 8.9 miles.

**Maps:** Ordnance Survey Landranger Sheet 194.

**Hills:** There is a testing hill at the end of the circular route.

**Surface:** A good part of this ride is on a bridleway, and a little on field paths. Although unsurfaced, the route seems to be well-drained even in winter.

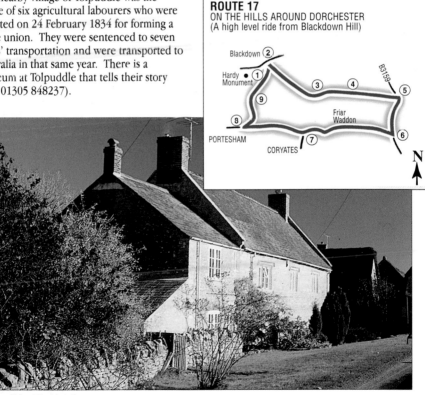

**ROUTE 17**
ON THE HILLS AROUND DORCHESTER
(A high level ride from Blackdown Hill)

*Above:* Friar Waddon farm.

**Safety:** There are no particular hazards associated with this route.

**Roads and Road Crossings:** There is a very short stretch of road at the beginning of the ride. If you take the circular option, then there is about 4 miles of quiet country lane with just the occasional car to bother you.

**Refreshments:** The Brewers Arms at Martinstown. There is plenty of choice in nearby Dorchester.

**Nearest Tourist Information Centre:** Unit 11, Antelope Walk, Dorchester, Dorset DT1 1BE (Tel: 01305 267992).

**Route Instructions:**

1. (0.0 miles): Leave the monument car park, turn right and descend the hill.

2. (0.1 miles): Take the second bridleway off to the right that is marked on the reverse side 'Inland Route Corton Hill' to climb a short, steep gravelly hill before you descend. Continue to follow the directions for 'Inland Route' from time to time passing through steel bar gates.

3. (1.6 miles): When under the first of three high-voltage power lines, cross the little concrete drive and proceed along the right-hand edge of the field (there is little obvious sign of the route on the ground). From the third power line the route becomes more obvious again.

4. (2.1 miles): Be careful when you come to a round barrow. The more obvious route goes to the right of the barrow, but you should swing left to access the gate that enables you to zigzag between the barrows.

5. (3.4 miles): Pass through a gate to meet the B3159. This point marks the end of the traffic-free ride, and if you are determined to stay completely traffic-free you should turn back. If you do not mind a little country traffic, turn right on to the B3159 and continue with the directions.

6. (4.2 miles): Turn right on to a quiet lane signposted 'Coryates 2 Portesham 4'.

7. (6.2 miles): At the junction, avoid the left turn and follow direction for Waddon and Portesham.

8. (7.5 miles): Turn right (almost back on yourself) to take the bridleway to Portesham Farm. Initially this is a very steep climb before you pass through the environs of the farm. After the farm, you climb a hill, pass through a gate and descend into a valley.

9. (8.2 miles): At the point where you are confronted by a plantation of conifers, take the route to the right and climb the steep hill to return to the car park.

10. (8.9 miles): Arrive back at the car park.

*Left:* The inland route to Corton Hill

# THE AXBRIDGE-CHEDDAR CYCLE WAY

The Cheddar Valley Railway Walk Society was formed in 1978 to create a walk and nature reserve along the disused railway line. The line — once known as the Strawberry Line because of the main goods that it carried in the summer months — was closed in 1963. There are beautiful views from the line over Cheddar Reservoir towards Wedmore Ridge and of course, closer to hand, there are views of the Mendip Hills and Cheddar Gorge.

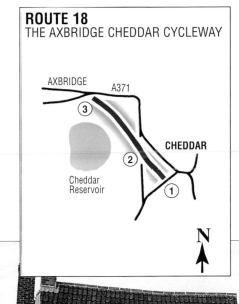

**ROUTE 18**
THE AXBRIDGE CHEDDAR CYCLEWAY

The Axbridge–Cheddar Cycleway Group is a branch of the railway walk society who have set up the cycleway in the last few months. Although short, the route is well constructed with fencing and safety barriers along the route. Work has been carried out by Sustrans.

**Background and Places of Interest**

### ● Cheddar Gorge

One of the best known limestone attractions in the British Isles. This immense chasm that splits the Mendip Hills is about 1½ miles long and in places the cliff walls approach 500ft high. Although the Somerset area was never directly affected by glaciation in the Ice Age periods, it did nevertheless experience Arctic conditions, during which underground drainage iced up. When the snow melted in the summer, there was an enormous surface flow of water which was responsible for cutting the gorge steadily deeper. The limestone in which the gorge is situated was laid down about 280 to 345 million years ago. Typical of limestone, it has strata and vertical fissures which form the stone into natural blocks. The earth's crust has suffered some

*Below:* The cobbled square, Axbridge.

distortion since the formation and this has caused the southerly dip in the rock of about 20 degrees. Although it is difficult in the summer months, try to experience the gorge when the road that runs through it is quiet, perhaps in the early morning or late evening. If that is not possible, use one of the public footpaths or the 274 steps of Jacob's Ladder to get to one of the spectacular viewpoints at Prospect Tower or Pulpit Rock.

### ● Cheddar Caves

As expected in a limestone region, there are many caves around the Mendip area. At the foot of the gorge there are two large caves that are open to the public — Gough's Cave and Cox's Cave. A visit to one of these will allow you to go deep below ground into the ancient limestone and see a range of stalactites, stalagmites and other colourful features which have built up over the last half a million years. More recently, cavemen lived in the entrance of Gough's Cave 12,000 years ago, and the bones of Ice Age animals including lion, hyena, mammoth and bison, have also been discovered in the caves. Also at the lower end of the gorge, a very large underground river emerges in the form of eighteen separate springs. Water is taken from this source and piped to Cheddar Reservoir — which you will see on the ride — for storage and from there as drinking water to houses in the area. Cheddar is also, of course, the home of Cheddar cheese. There are several places where you can visit and see cheese made in the traditional way. The Cheddar Gorge Cheese Company claims to be the place where the only real Cheddar-made Cheddar cheese in the world comes from (Tel: 01934 742810).

### ● Axbridge

This is a pleasant old town whose market square has been cobbled and where you can pleasantly while away an hour or two. The earliest mention of Axbridge was in the 10th century when a fort was built to defend the area against Viking raiders. It is thought that the market place developed outside the northern gate of the fort. The borough was established as a commercial centre in 1229 when a charter was granted by Henry III freeing the burgesses from the payment of tolls.

*Left:* Axbridge.

*Left:* Cheddar.

**Distance:** 1.2 miles (2.4-mile round trip).

**Maps:** Ordnance Survey Landranger Sheet 182.

**Hills:** None.

**Surface:** Very good stone-based surface varying from 4–12ft wide.

**Safety:** There are no hazards on this ride.

**Roads and Road Crossings:** There are no road crossings on this short ride. However, the route stops short of both Cheddar and Axbridge and the roads into these two towns are fairly busy.

**Refreshments:** Cheddar is a tourist trap and has plenty of places where you can spend your money. Axbridge is a very pleasant and comparatively unspoilt town with a couple of nice looking pubs — the Axbridge Lion and the Lamb — and a tea room or two.

**Nearest Tourist Information Centre:** The Gorge, Cheddar, Somerset BS27 3QE (Tel: 01934 744071) (Not open all year).

**Starting Point:** It is a ½ mile to the start of the ride. Leave the car park via Roynon Way. Then turn right to follow the A371 past the Bath Arms Hotel and take the B3151 towards Wedmore by turning left at the war memorial. Then turn right as directed by the blue cycleway sign, also signposted to Valley Line Industrial Park.

**Parking and Toilets:** Park in Cheddar at the pay and display car park at Budgens Supermarket.

**Route Instructions:**

1. (0.0 miles): Pass around the steel barrier to cycle between wire link fence.

2. (0.2 miles): Leave the section that runs at the foot of gardens, to enter the old railway line proper, and pass through an area of sports pitches.

3. (1.2 miles): The route emerges at the road into Axbridge.

# THE BRIDGWATER AND TAUNTON CANAL
*(Bridgwater to Lower Maunsel)*

The canal has a total length of 15½ miles and was opened in 1827. It was part of a scheme to create a route between Exeter and Bristol. The canal brought coal and iron to the settlements of Somerset via the River Parrett This ride can be linked with Ride No 20 to make a continuous route between Bridgwater and Taunton. It is a beautifully quiet canal where you will be extremely unlucky if you meet more than a handful of people on the towpath. As the right to cycle is permissive, strictly speaking a cycle permit is required. This is obtainable from the Waterway Manager, South Wales and Somerset Canals, Canal Office, The Wharf, Govilon, Abergavenny, Gwent NP7 9NY (Tel: 01873 830328), or by calling at Maunsel Canal Centre, Maunsel Lock Cottage, Banklands, North Newton, Bridgwater, Somerset TA7 0DH (Tel:  01278 663160). The canal centre is open between 9.00am and 5.00pm May to September.

**Background and Places of Interest**

● **Bridgwater**
The docks were opened in 1841 and it was at one time the fifth largest port in Great Britain. They were originally built to provide ships on the River Parrett with a safe shelter. The water in the dock was maintained by high tide in the River Parrett, and the water was retained behind the large lock gates. There were two locks: a large ship lock and a smaller barge lock and these were blocked off when the dock was closed in 1971. Fortunately, the barge lock is working again and the canal is now connected with the inland waterways system via the Bristol Channel and the Gloucester and Sharpness Canal.

● **Admiral Blake Museum**
You will find the name of Admiral Robert Blake everywhere in Bridgwater; streets are named after him, so are pubs and so is the museum.  Cromwell's General at Sea was the

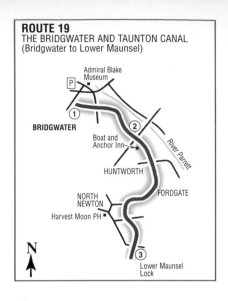

**ROUTE 19**
THE BRIDGWATER AND TAUNTON CANAL
(Bridgwater to Lower Maunsel)

first great seaman to have the honour of a grand funeral in Westminster Abbey.  When Spain lost its sea power, the gap was filled by the Dutch.  He fought the Dutch from the Hebrides to the English Channel.  The fortunes of war went up and down; first the Dutch forced Blake into the Thames and swept the channel with a broom at their admiral's mast head; then the English gained the upper hand over a battle of four days. Admiral Blake was also involved in campaigns in the Mediterranean and the West Indies when his fleet took the island of Jamaica, marking the start of a worldwide struggle. His last and greatest feat was the destruction of the whole Spanish fleet in Tenerife, where not a single ship escaped and all were sunk or burnt.  The admiral was reputedly a very popular figure as he did his best to make his sailors' lives more bearable.  A main attraction of the museum is a display of Sedgemoor battle relics.  The Admiral Blake Museum, Blake Street, Bridgwater (Tel: 01278 456127).

● **The Battle of Sedgemoor**
The climax of the rebellion led by the Duke of Monmouth against his uncle James II took place 3 miles south east of Bridgwater along the A372.  A track is signposted and leads from Westonzoyland to the position where the Royal Camp is thought to have been placed.

*Right:* Homely accommodation by the canal.

*Above:* The Bridgwater & Taunton Canal has some idyllic scenes.

**Starting Point:** This is ½ mile from the car park. From the Market Street Car Park, turn right at the mini-roundabout. At the traffic lights marking the crossroads, carry straight on taking great care. Gain access to the canal towpath by turning left immediately after the wall which screens the canal; this is opposite a small parade of shops.

**Parking and Toilets:** Park at the pay and display car park at Market Street, opposite the Mecca Leisure Cinema and where all-day parking is reasonably priced and free on Sundays. There are public toilets a few yards from the cinema.

**Distance:** 6.4 miles (12.8 mile round trip).

**Maps:** Ordnance Survey Landranger Sheets 182 and 193.

**Hills:** None.

**Surface:** The towpath varies from well-surfaced to grassy sections. In the summer, it would appear to be fully cycleable, but the unsurfaced sections could become muddy in the winter months.

**Safety:** Beside the normal hazard associated with arched canal bridges, some of the bridges coming out of Bridgwater are lower than normal.

**Roads and Road Crossings:** There are no significant road crossings.

**Refreshments:** Plenty of choice in Bridgwater where most places are named after Admiral Robert Blake. There is also the Boat and Anchor Inn at canalside at Huntworth, the Harvest Moon at North Newton.

**Nearest Tourist Information Centre:**
50 High Street, Bridgwater, Somerset TA6 3BL (Tel: 01278 427652) (Not open all year).

**Route Instructions:**

It is a very simple matter to cycle the towpath and no detailed directions are required.

1. (0.0 miles): Descend the ramp from the road to gain access to the canal towpath on the right-hand side of the canal by West Street Bridge, beyond which massive timber baulks support the high retaining walls.

2. (1.4 miles): Using the bridge, switch to the left side of the canal.

3. (6.4 miles): The end of the ride is at Lower Maunsel Lock where there is an old lock keeper's cottage, and morning coffee and ice cream are available. There is also a landscaped car park and a picnic site set in an old orchard.

*Below:* Leaving Bridgwater.

# THE BRIDGWATER AND TAUNTON CANAL
*(Taunton to Lower Maunsel)*

**Background and Places of Interest**

### ROUTE 20
THE BRIDGWATER AND TAUNTON CANAL
(Taunton to Lower Maunsel)

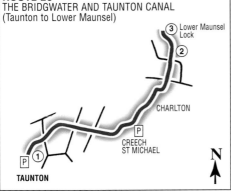

This canal is an absolute gem. It is unspoilt, quiet, full of wildlife and seems not to have been discovered by cyclists. There are plans to surface parts of the towpath where there is no sensible alternative quiet road. The section to Creech St Michael is already done and the next section to Charlton is to be done in the near future, but there are no current plans to surface from Charlton to North Newton. The gates on the towpath are very sensible and convenient for the cyclist as they have a 'V-shaped' slot which you can pass through without unfastening the gate. As the right to cycle is permissive, strictly speaking a cycle permit is required. This is obtainable from the Waterway Manager, South Wales and Somerset Canals, Canal Office, The Wharf, Govilon, Abergavenny, Gwent NP7 9NY (Tel: 01873 830328), or by calling at Maunsel Canal Centre, Maunsel Lock Cottage, Banklands, North Newton, Bridgwater, Somerset TA7 0DH (Tel: 01278 663160). The canal centre is open between 9.00am and 5.00pm May to September. The first road that you encounter is not until Durston, by which time you will have already cycled seven miles and even this is an extremely quiet country lane. The ride ends at an attractive picnic site about half-way along the canal, so why not take a picnic? Alternatively, if you are feeling really energetic then you could continue all the way to Bridgwater.

### ● The Bridgwater and Taunton Canal
In the early 1800s, canals represented the most effective method of transporting heavy goods and several schemes were proposed for linking the Bristol Channel with the English Channel, in part to avoid the need to navigate around Land's End. Due no doubt to the railways, the grand plan was never completed, but two elements — the Grand Western Canal and the B&T Canal — were built. Opposition to the canal came from the Conservators of the River Tone, but it eventually opened in 1827. The opening of the Grand Western Canal Somerset Line linked Taunton and Tiverton in 1838. The junction with the GWC is immediately next to the canal bridge at the start of the ride. As is usually the story, the B&T came under railway control in 1866 and the GWC Somerset Line ceased operation in 1869.

*Below:* Taunton Castle.

Traffic ceased on the B&T in 1907 and in 1963 it was taken over by the British Waterways Board. The B&T has recently been restored by the BWB, Somerset County Council, Taunton Deane Borough Council and Sedgemoor District Council.

## ● Taunton

Somerset's county town is set in its own rich vale notable for its orchards and pasture. In the 14th century the town was famous for its serge (a durable worsted fabric) and was a prosperous wool town. It gives the impression of busy prosperity and it has been featured in many periods of English history from when King Ina defended the area from the fortified banks of the River Tone, to the Civil War and the Monmouth Rebellion when the town took a determined anti-royalist stance. Taunton Castle was where the 'Bloody Assize' took place when the

notorious Judge Jeffreys tried over 500 supporters of the Monmouth Rebellion. It is also the site where the last ever trial of witchcraft took place. If you have time you will be able to spend a very pleasant day in Taunton.

## ● Somerset Cricket Museum

You may not realise it but the high fence next to the suggested car park marks the home of Somerset County Cricket Ground. The club has a very colourful history with such stars as Viv Richards, Martin Crowe, Steve Waugh and Jimmy Cook. The museum is next to the County Ground and is normally open from 10.00am until 4.00pm, but ring to confirm between October and March (Tel: 01823 275893).

*Below:* Leaving Taunton.

**Starting Point:** This is immediately by the Coal Orchard Car Park.

**Parking and Toilets:** I parked at the pay and display Coal Orchard Car Park. Costs are reasonable and it is free on a Sunday. Priory Bridge Car Park is close by and equally suitable. It is also possible to do the ride the other way round: park at Lower Maunsel picnic site and ride into Taunton.

**Distance:** 7.5 miles (15-mile round trip).

**Maps:** Ordnance Survey Landranger Sheet 193.

**Hills:** None.

**Surface:** The towpath has several variations between a broad stone-based track of 9ft width to a soft grassy surface. In the summer months it is fully cycleable, but in the winter the grassy sections could become muddy.

**Safety:** Care should be taken when cycling under canal bridges as their curved nature and narrowing of the towpath could lead to a nasty blow on the head or a thorough wetting. Also, one or two of the bridges are a little on the low side.

**Roads and Road Crossings:** Only one tiny length of road at the end of the ride.

**Refreshments:** There are many pubs and cafés in Taunton. There are also two pubs in Bathpool, two at Creech St Michael and the Railway Hotel at Outwood.

**Nearest Tourist Information Centre:** The Library, Corporation Street, Taunton, Somerset TA1 4AN (Tel: 01823 274785).

**Route Instructions:**

1. (0.0 miles): With the car park behind you and facing Safeway's, turn right to follow the River Tone and after about 500yd turn left over the narrow concrete bridge with the black railings, walk over the two weirs and join the canal at Firepool Lock.

2. (7.2 miles): Join a quiet country lane for a short distance, by passing through the white gate/barrier, and then pass through a similar gate/barrier to rejoin the towpath.

3. (7.5 miles): The ride ends at Lower Maunsel Lock where there is an old lock keeper's cottage, and morning coffee and ice cream are available. There is a landscaped car park and picnic site set in an old orchard.

# EGGESFORD FOREST
*(A circular route in the forest)*

*I arrived at Eggesford Station a little after four, and found there Lord Portsmouth's brougham waiting to take me to the house, so there was no trouble at all. The scenery here is so lovely and the house very handsome...*
Thomas Hardy in 1885

This ride takes advantage of one of the two waymarked trails in the Eggesford Forest area. This one is in Heywood Wood and the other is in nearby Flashdown Wood. It is possible to link them together using a short on-road section. The waymarking is not entirely reliable but on the whole is good. The problem with forests, though, is the lack of landmarks. Once you lose your way in the forest, you are prone to ever-increasing disorientation, so an Ordnance Survey map or one of the free route leaflets available from Eggesford Country Centre would be a valuable ally in case some of the waymarkers have disappeared. Heywood was planted in 1920 and is specifically run for both timber production and recreation. It is the finest wood in the area and has magnificent trees and marvellous views of the surrounding countryside.

## Background and Places of Interest

### ● Eggesford Forest
Eggesford is situated in the heart of Devon; an area of rolling hills, forests, fast flowing rocky rivers and soil that can be as red as claret. The Forestry Commission was formed just after World War 1 in 1919 and the very first planting of trees was undertaken by the Commission in Eggesford in that

*Right:* Towards North Down plantation.

**ROUTE 21**
EGGESFORD
(A circular route in the Forest)

Tarka Line

Heywood Wood

Eggesford Station

A377

2

1

E Flashdown Wood

D

C

B

A

Eggesford Country Centre

N

same year on 8 December. The purpose of the Commission is to manage the forest estate owned by the nation and it is good to see some waymarked trails for cyclists who often seem not to be as welcome as walkers or horseriders in other Forestry Commission areas. The area is alive with wildlife — the River Taw attracts herons, kingfishers and dippers. In the summer months chiffchaffs, tree creepers and wood pigeons are abundant in the woods, with wrens and yellowhammers in the hedgerows and that habitually soaring, slightly sinister bird that is a stranger to most visitors from South East England visiting Devon or Cornwall — the buzzard.

## ● Eggesford

In prehistoric times the Taw Valley was a thickly wooded impenetrable area and was not settled until the Saxon era, and some valley clearance was undertaken at that time. The original settlement was based on the river crossing at the ford near Heywood Wood. You will cycle past the remains of a Norman motte and bailey castle that was intended to control the crossing point at the northern end of Heywood. Latter-day Eggesford is a mile upstream where All Saints' Church and the original Eggesford House stood, part of which is now Eggesford Garden Centre. This centre is unusual in that it is also the home of the Eggesford Country Centre as well.

## ● The Tarka Line

It may seem strange at first that all trains stop at Eggesford Station, when virtually nobody appears to live there. This is because the local landowner made it a condition of releasing the land that enabled the railway to be built. The line which runs for 39 miles between Exeter and Barnstaple follows the gentle valley of the Yeo and Taw. Its history is complex as several railway companies have been involved. The first stretch to open was the Exeter to Crediton Railway in 1851; this was extended by an additional stretch which was operated by the North Devon Railway in 1854. Eventually the line was taken over by the London and South Western Railway Company which in turn became the Southern Railway, who operated the legendary 'Atlantic Coast Express' to the North Devon and Cornwall coast.

*Above:* Eggesford station.

**Starting Point:** In Heywood Forest close to the Wembworthy Centre (a Devon CC outdoor centre for school and youth groups). If you have parked at the garden centre, you will need to leave the car park (Point A), turn left (Point B) away from the church, when you meet the narrow road (Point C) turn right and go downhill for a short distance and then turn left (Point D) as directed to 'Wembworthy 13/4, Winkleigh 4' to embark on a steep climb. Turn right as directed to Wembworthy Centre (Point E) and then almost immediately left. The route starts here.

**Parking and Toilets:** Park at Eggesford Garden Centre, home of Eggesford Country Centre, where there are toilets.

**Distance:** If you cycle from the country centre (which is the practical way to do it) the distance there and back is 6 miles. The off-road ride around Heywood Wood which is the feature of this chapter is 3 miles. There is a further possible ride on a waymarked trail around Flashdown Wood. If you include this on your return to the country centre the overall distance will be approximately 6.3 miles.

**Maps:** Ordnance Survey Landranger Sheets 180 and 191.

**Hills:** There are several short steep climbs.

**Surface:** The going is wide, unsurfaced and a little rough in places, but would appear to be fairly firm over most of its length throughout the year.

**Safety:** If you cycle from the Eggesford Country Centre, be careful of the traffic on the Wembworthy road.

**Roads and Road Crossings:** There is one stretch of quiet lane at the end of the circular route in Heywood Wood.

**Refreshments:** Excellent refreshment facilities at the Eggesford Country Centre. There is also the Fox and Hounds Hotel just north of Eggesford on the A377.

**Cycle Hire:** Eggesford Country Cycle Hire at the country centre is open 7 days a week for the whole year round (Tel: 01769 580250).

*Right:* Eggesford Forest.

**Nearest Tourist Information Centre:** Market Street Car Park, Market Street, Crediton, Devon EX17 2BN (Tel: 01363 772006).

**Route Instructions:**
Little direction is needed through Heywood Wood, just generally follow the brown cycle trail signs. On your way around you will see the earthen ramparts of a Norman castle. There are also some unusual specimen trees *en route* — a large Douglas fir, a huge Chile pine (monkey puzzle tree) and a Western red cedar.

1. (0.0 miles): Take the off-road route as indicated by the brown cycle trail sign (also indicated as a public footpath).

2. (2.5 miles): Rejoin a country lane and return to the starting point.

3. (3.0 miles): Back at the start point.

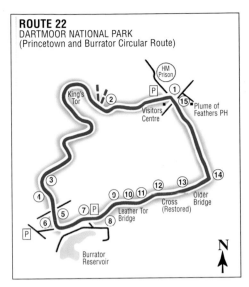

**ROUTE 22**
DARTMOOR NATIONAL PARK
(Princetown and Burrator Circular Route)

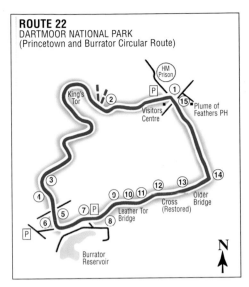

Within the map: HM Prison · King's Tor · Visitors Centre · Plume of Feathers PH · Leather Tor Bridge · Cross (Restored) · Older Bridge · Burrator Reservoir · N

# DARTMOOR NATIONAL PARK
*(Princetown and Burrator Circular Route)*

This is the wildest route in the book but also one of the most enjoyable as it is so varied. Initially the ride follows a disused railway line across wild open moorland and then passes through varied woodland and over rocky and challenging bridlepaths. You will enjoy magnificent views of tors, woodland and the large Burrator Reservoir. The route divides conveniently into three: the first section follows the track of the old Great Western Railway (Yelverton to Princetown line);

the second is tough going, being uphill and very stony (the Dartmoor National Park publicity leaflet describes it as an interesting technical ride!); and the third is a recently surfaced bridleway which provides an excellent finishing section. I cycled the full circular route of 13 miles, but towards the end of the old railway line there are several stiles and I feel that these, together with the tough second sections would make the ride too arduous for young children and the less fit. I would therefore recommend two possibilities: either ride the old railway line to Point 3 and then return, or start the route in reverse and cycle to Point 14 and then return.

**Background and Places of Interest**

● **Princetown**

There are not many places in England that are truly sinister, but the prison in Princetown is certainly one of them. Even on a day without the normal swirling mist and driving rain, and with the sun shining, it still appears to be full of foreboding. It is, I believe, the greyest place in the world. The building of those awful drab walls was commenced in 1806 by French prisoners of war who were effectively forced to build their own gaol. Those poor souls must have hated every Englishman they saw. Later, in 1812, the French were joined by

*Below:* The bridleway back to Princetown.

over two hundred captured American sailors. Their contribution to this free building programme was the completion of the church already started by the French. It has a beautiful east window that lights up the drab grey walls and was donated by American women in memory of their countryfolk who died there. The prison attracts many visitors to the town who, with their cameras and tourist trappings, come to take photographs of the prison and hope to see a work party of prisoners undertaking their task. In the centre of the town is the Dartmoor National Park Visitor Centre, which is well worth a visit if you wish to learn more about Dartmoor.

### ● Burrator Reservoir

Below the rocky crag of Sheepstor lies the reservoir that supplies the city of Plymouth. It is thought that Sir Francis Drake constructed the first leat that carried drinking water to Plymouth, and you will cross it twice on your ride. It is known as Devonport Leat and provides a picturesque picnic stop. On your ride you will occasionally see posts inscribed PCWW; these mark the limits of the rain catchment area for the Plymouth City Water Works. At the annual Fishinge Feaste at

Burrator, the mayor's toast includes a wish 'May the descendants of him who brought us water never want wine'.

### ● Tavistock

A pleasant market town and the birthplace of Sir Francis Drake — a fact that you will not be allowed to forget if you visit there, and that is perhaps how it should be. Arguably he was the greatest man that England ever produced. Born in an age when Englishmen were isolated on their little island, by the end of his life he had terrified our enemies and ensured that there was no navy or ship that would willingly contemplate challenging a British ship at sea. Tavistock is a Saxon name meaning a stockade established on the River Tavy, but the place was insignificant until a Benedictine abbey was established there in the 10th century. The abbey became enormously wealthy and when tin was discovered in the 12th century, Tavistock became one of three stannary towns on the edge of Dartmoor. The others were Ashburton and Chagford and it was to these towns that the tinners brought their metal ingots to be tested and sold. The tin was mined out by the beginning of the 17th century, but after that there was a considerable trade in copper.

**Starting Point:** It is best to start at Princetown so that you can enjoy refreshments at the beginning or end of your ride. The ride starts from Princetown car park *(see below)*. Alternatively, you can start at Cross Gate.

**Parking and Toilets:** Park in Princetown car park. The charges are very reasonable, just £1 per day. There is a small free car parking area at Cross Gate.

**Distance:** The complete circular route is 12.9 miles but if you prefer to ride the railway line as far as the stile and back it is about 12 miles, or if you ride the bridleway on to the moor and back it is 3.8 miles.

**Maps:** Ordnance Survey Landranger Sheets 191, 201 and 202 (the route sits on the corner of all three). Alternatively, Ordnance Survey Outdoor Leisure Map 28 covers the whole ride using one sheet.

**Hills:** There is a long and arduous climb from Burrator Reservoir on to the moor.

**Surface:** The disused railway section is best, being very wide and well drained. It appears that little has been done to it since the track was lifted. Consequently, it lacks the binding effect that a grit top dressing would provide and loose stones can be troublesome if you go too fast. The middle section, on the bridleway that leaves Burrator, is very rough going with very large stones. The final section on the resurfaced bridleway that leads you back to Princetown in a northerly direction is easy going with just the transverse drainage gulleys to watch out for.

**Safety:** Care should be taken when coming off the railway embankment to cross the B3212. On a ride such as this a helmet is important and so are the right clothes. The weather can change very quickly on Dartmoor and a day that starts out fine and sunny can quickly change into very bad weather, so take warm and waterproof clothing if there is any chance of bad weather, and listen to the weather forecast before you go.

**Roads and Road Crossings:** Be careful where the old railway crosses the B3212 as you have to descend from the embankment.

**Refreshments:** The Plume of Feathers and the Devil's Elbow are in the centre of Princetown, together with Lords Restaurant and a fish and chip shop housed in the old police station.

**Cycle Hire:** Family Cycle Hire, Peak Hill Farm, Yelverton (Tel: 01822 852908); Tavistock Cycles (Tel: 01822 617630); Canal Leisure Cycle Hire (Tel:01822 833651).

**Nearest Tourist Information Centre:** Town Hall, Bedford Square, Tavistock, Devon PL19 0AE (Tel: 01822 612938) (Not open all year).

**Route Instructions:**

1. (0.0 miles): Turn left from the car park to follow signs for the Tyrwhitt Trail. Immediately after the fire station turn left as directed for 'Disused Railway'.

2. (1.7 miles ): At the fork in the route (there are in fact three possible routes) take the left-most possible one to take you around King's Tor.

3. (6.0 miles): You now come to the first stile, which marks the interface between the moorland and field systems. You need to lift the bike over this (and there are four more to follow, I'm afraid).

4. (6.4 miles): A further stile/gate/gate-combination to overcome a missing bridge, and from there you pass through a stile and then two more gates until you have to carefully descend the embankment to cross the B3212.

5. (6.9 miles): Cross the road with great care and climb the steps and stile on the other side.

6. (7.0 miles): Negotiate a further stile (the last) to enter a field leading down to a narrow lane; turn left on to the lane (there are good views of Burrator to be had away to the right).

7. (8.0 miles): Where the lane veers off to the right at Cross Gate (just before a cross also on the right) take the shingly track left; there is a small car park here.

8. (8.2 miles): Cross Devonport Leat to go downhill, avoiding the temptation to follow the line of the leat.

9. (8.6 miles): Cross another watercourse by Leather Tor Bridge and immediately after bear right to climb the hill.

10. (9.0 miles): At what could be loosely called a T-junction, turn left to continue with a stone wall on your left marking the woodland area and open moorland on the right.

11. (9.3 miles): Enter the open moorland through the gate and this is where the going gets rough.

12. (10.2 miles): Pass a cross on the right.

13. (10.6 miles): Ford a small stream and cross Older Bridge (the Devonport Leat again).

14. (11.0 miles): At the crossing of ways turn left to take the nicely surfaced bridleway in the direction of the North Hessary Tor transmitting station, that takes you to the Plume of Feathers.

15. (12.8 miles): Cross the road at the Plume of Feathers to return to the car park.

16. (12.9 miles): Arrive at the car park.

*Below:* Devonport Leat.

# THE PLYM VALLEY CYCLE TRAIL
*(Goodameavy to Laira Bridge)*

We have Sustrans and Devon County Council to thank for this outstanding ride that takes you from the edge of Dartmoor almost into Plymouth. Parts of the Plym Valley have been the scene of industrial activity since the 16th century, with tin, iron, lead, silver and copper being mined, and china clay, arsenic and slate being quarried. Wood, paper and tanning mills were powered from the readily available timber and water of the valley. The ride mostly follows the route of the old Great Western Railway and the views are spectacular as you follow the Plym Valley over huge stone viaducts, bridges and a tunnel that thankfully have not suffered the fate of demolition as has been the case on so many other old railway lines. In fact, if I were given the task of giving this ride a name, I would have called it the Viaduct Trail.

## Background and Places of Interest

● **South Devon and Tavistock Railway.**
This part of the Great Western Railway began life as the South Devon and Tavistock Railway in 1859, and like many other great engineering projects in the West Country was overseen by the engineer Brunel. It was built as a link between Tavistock and Plymouth and was part of the transport corridor which developed in the Plym Valley to link the many industries there with the harbours of Plymouth. Cycling through Shaugh Tunnel is an interesting experience (especially if you have failed to bring lights). It is 308yd long and Brunel in his first report to the railway company reported that the tunnel was causing problems, 'the ground not proving favourable for rapid progress'. The viaducts which you pass over really are something special. There are four of them altogether: the first at Ham Green is the longest with excellent views across Bickleigh Vale and the edge of Dartmoor; the second is

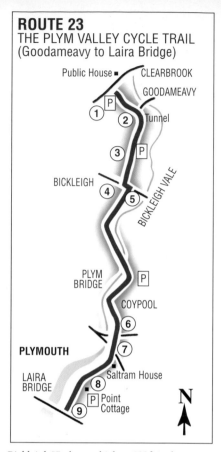

## ROUTE 23
### THE PLYM VALLEY CYCLE TRAIL
(Goodameavy to Laira Bridge)

Bickleigh Viaduct, which at 123ft is the highest and boasts seven arches spanning a steep-sided valley. Riverford Viaduct is next and stands 97ft high. It has five arches and replaced an earlier wooden structure. The final one is Cann Viaduct which overlooks a scene which in times past was filled with considerable industrial activity.

● **Saltram House**
This ride takes you through the grounds of Saltram House. This is National Trust property and one of the largest houses in Devon and was constructed in George II's reign by a member of the Bagg family, who had the nickname of 'Bottomless Bagg' due to his well-known greed. It has magnificent interior plasterwork and decoration with two rooms by Robert Adam and portraits by Sir Joshua Reynolds. It is complete with its original contents and is set in a landscaped

park of 300 acres overlooking the Plym Estuary. It is open from 1 April to 31 October. (Tel: 01752 336546 for opening times of the house and gardens.)

## ● Plymouth

Plymouth is the largest city in Devon and is really a combination of three towns: Devonport in the west on the banks of the River Tamar, Stonehouse in the middle and Sutton in the east. It contains many attractions of its own, with its Elizabethan Barbican, historic waterfront and modern city centre; but any visitor to Plymouth will find themselves drawn as if by a magnet to the Hoe, where Drake played that famous game of bowls. Here you will find Smeaton's Tower, the city's best known landmark, which was originally built on Eddystone Rock in 1789 and was moved stone by stone to the Hoe in 1884. If you have time, climb to the top where you will enjoy the most magnificent views of Drake's Island which was fortified in the 16th century and has been used as a prison and is now an adventure-training centre.

**Starting Point:** Clearbrook Car Park.

**Parking and Toilets**: There is a car park conveniently situated at Clearbrook, and the ride is described from that point. There is also a small car park just south of Shaugh Tunnel which may suit you if you are nervous of tunnels, and one at Plym Bridge. There is a further car park close to Point Cottage at the entrance to Saltram House grounds.

**Distance:** 8.5 miles (17-mile round trip).

**Maps:** Ordnance Survey Landranger Sheet 201.

**Hills:** One minor one where you leave the old railway line in Bickleigh.

**Surface:** Wide and stone-based with grit dressing.

**Safety:** Due to the length and curved nature of Shaugh Tunnel, you are truly unable to 'see the light at the end of the tunnel', so you must bring a cycle lamp or torch, or you will have to travel a short distance in darkness.

*Above:* On the edge of the moor at Clearbrook.

**Roads and Road Crossings:** The first mile of this ride is on a quiet country lane from Clearbrook Car Park to the point near Goodameavy where you will join the trail. There is a section of ½ mile through the village of Bickleigh, and limited road work at Coypool.

**Refreshments:** Not a lot of choice; there is a pub in Clearbrook which looks fine and possibilities in Plym Bridge.

**Nearest Tourist Information Centre:** Island House, 9 The Barbican, Plymouth, Devon PL1 2LS (Tel: 01752 264849).

**Route Instructions:**

1. (0.0 miles): From the car park you will find the direction to the Plym Valley Cycle Trail clearly marked on a blue finger with a cycle logo.

2. (0.8 miles): By the little green barrier, you will find a green signboard describing the route of the Plym Valley Cycle Trail and marking its start; after a short distance you will enter Shaugh Tunnel, switch your front light on!

3. (2.2 miles): Turn right (as directed for the Plym Valley Cycle Trail) when you meet a minor lane.

4. (2.6 miles): Turn left (again as directed) at the T-junction.

5. (2.7 miles): Rejoin the cycle trail by turning right; there are marvellous views of Bickleigh Vale at this point.

6. (6.2 miles): At Coypool, by the Royal Marines depot, join a road and after a few yards you will come to a 'Give Way' junction. Carry straight on as directed to 'Cycle Path to Laira Bridge', and follow alongside the single track railway line.

7. (6.5 miles): Pass under the A38 flyover, and enjoy a wide open grassy embankment for a while before entering a wooded area.

8. (7.7 miles): After enjoying the estate of Saltram House, leave the grounds by Point Cottage.

9. (8.5 miles): Arrive at Laira Bridge and the busy outskirts of Plymouth.

*Below:* Plymouth Hoe.

*Bottom:* Bickleigh.

# THE TARKA TRAIL

*(Petrockstowe to East-the-Water)*

North Devon has changed its name over recent years and is now marketed very effectively as Tarka Country. In addition to the Tarka Trail, the railway line from Exeter to Barnstaple is the Tarka Line and even one of the local brews of the Tally Ho Brewery at Hatherleigh is known as Tarka's Tipple. The Tarka Trail is a 180-mile footpath which plots the journeys of *Tarka the Otter* written by Henry Williamson. Part of this long distance route is a traffic-free cycle path of 30 miles or so that runs around the Taw/Torridge Estuary from Braunton to Petrockstowe. This ride is one of two in this book that utilises the Tarka Trail; the other runs from Bideford to Barnstaple. One of the most attractive features is that a Bike Bus is provided (DevonBus Service 361) that enables you to undertake a one-way journey and be returned to your starting point. The bus can carry up to six bikes in a specially converted section at the rear, and operates every day except Wednesday. For example you could ride to East-the-Water, cross the bridge to Bideford and be collected at either 1310 or 1710 and come back on the bus with your bike to Petrockstowe. Alternatively, you could cycle the whole route to Barnstaple and be returned. For further information telephone Devon County Council's DevonBus enquiry line (Tel: 01392 or 01271 or 01752 382800).

*Below:* The River Torridge

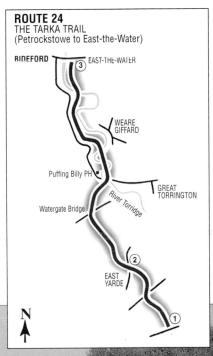

**ROUTE 24**
THE TARKA TRAIL
(Petrockstowe to East-the-Water)

BIDEFORD — EAST-THE-WATER
③
WEARE GIFFARD
Puffing Billy PH
GREAT TORRINGTON
Watergate Bridge
River Torridge
②
EAST YARDE
①
N

## Background and Places of Interest

### ● Tarka the Otter

Amongst best known of all animal stories, *Tarka the Otter* was published in 1927, and with over 30 editions now issued it has become an international classic. It is set in an area that has changed little in recent years and which provides a home to the present-day otter population which after many years of decline this century due to pollution, has now been reintroduced successfully to many rivers in this country. However, it needs to be said that the chance of seeing an otter is very unlikely as they are shy creatures. According to the author Henry Williamson, the name Tarka was Celtic for little water wanderer, and he travelled extensively through the 'land of the two rivers' chasing salmon, avoiding the hunts and looking after his future mate.

### ● Hatherleigh

A beautiful small market town with narrow winding streets and picturesque cottages with a very old public house, the George, which is worth coming many miles to see. In addition to the George, there is also a well-respected micro-brewery in the town where the staff will show you round and explain their brewing processes. They have originated the most imaginative of names for their brews: Potboilers Brew, Nutters, Thurgia, Jollop,

Master Jack's Mild, not forgetting of course Tarka's Tipple. The brewery is situated at the rear of the Tally Ho Country Inn, in the old town bakery and has a capacity of 260 gallons of real ales per week (Tel: 01837 810306 for information). There is also a village pottery where work can not only be bought but also seen in progress (Tel: 01837 810624).

### ● Great Torrington

This is a hilltop town whose attractive inner parts are hidden from the passing motorist. Visitors are wise if they find the town centre and explore it for themselves. Around three sides of Torrington is an open common, and people who have visited the Holy Land have spoken of it as the English Jerusalem. It has several industries including the Dartington Crystal Glass Factory which was established in the 1960s and is a major success story, providing employment and training in an area of rural depopulation. Also worthy of a visit is Rosemoor Garden which belongs to the Royal Horticultural Society. It now consists of two gardens; the first was presented to the RHS by Lady Anne Palmer and it is a place of interest at all times of the year. It is internationally renowned and is frequently featured on television. The new National Garden is an additional 32 acres of fields which has been donated to the RHS and is gradually taking shape to represent many varied aspects of gardening.

*Above:* The Puffing Billy at Torrington.

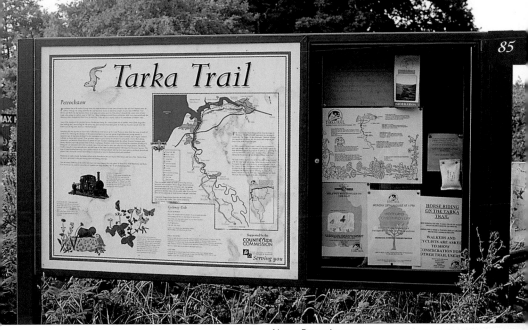

**Starting Point:** The car park at Petrockstowe. Beware if you carry your cycles on the roof of your car or you will end up with a fine mess, as the headroom as you enter the car park is restricted to 7ft 3in.

**Parking and Toilets:** I parked at Petrockstowe. It is also possible to park at East Yarde, Watergate, Torrington (toilets also available), Loxdown, Cross and East-the-Water where toilets are also available.

**Distance:** 13 miles from Petrockstowe to the railway station and visitor centre at East-the-Water, using the Bike Bus to return. Alternatively, a 26-mile round trip.

**Maps:** Ordnance Survey Landranger Sheets 180 and 191.

**Hills:** None.

**Surface:** A very good stone-based track.

**Safety:** No particular hazards. There is a short tunnel to pass through but light is not a problem.

**Roads and Road Crossings:** Some minor roads are crossed, but with no real hazards.

**Refreshments:** The Puffing Billy at Torrington in the old station, and plenty of choice at Bideford.

*Above:* Petrockstowe.

**Cycle Hire:** Bideford Cycle Hire (Tel: 01237 424123).

**Nearest Tourist Information Centre:** Victoria Park, The Quay, Bideford, Devon EX39 2QQ (Tel: 01237 477676/421853).

**Route Instructions:**

This is an extremely well-marked route and virtually no directions are required. The Tarka Trail is indicated by a blue arrow with an otter footprint superimposed.

1. (0.0 miles): Head north by leaving the car park to join the road and then take the cycle path that passes through the wooden five-bar gates.

2. (3.3 miles): At East Yarde Car Park, cross the road and take the route through the small wooden five-bar gate to pass through the small thicket of trees.

3. (13.1 miles): Arrive at the Information Centre, housed in a carriage at the old Bideford station.

# THE CAIRN NATURE RESERVE AND OLD RAILWAY PATH
*(Ilfracombe to Lee Bridge)*

*Grandest old place in the world it be,*
*Dear old Ilfracombe by the sea.*

This ride takes your through The Cairn, which is now a woodland nature reserve, and along the route of the old Barnstaple to Ilfracombe Railway. It is really intended as a walk, but having said that, the trackbed has been re-laid and topped with fine stone and makes an ideal cycleway. The Devon Trust for Nature Conservation are content for cyclists to ride on it 'within reason'. It is one of the most beautiful stretches of disused railway I have come across and winds its way gently through the countryside. It takes you through a short tunnel — no lights required — and past two reservoirs. Old railway lines like these, although narrow, are a valuable medium for wildlife. Even in late summer it was smothered in wild flowers and completely taken over by hordes of Red Admiral butterflies. There are fine views to be had, north to the Bristol Channel and beyond that the Welsh coast. To the west there is a fine range of hills known as The Torrs that mark the coastline.

## Background and Places of Interest

### ● The Cairn

A century ago, The Cairn was 20 acres of rough hill grazing with rocky outcrops. In 1911 it was planted with a good mixture of deciduous and coniferous trees and converted to a country park laid out with walks. It is now a woodland nature reserve and leased from the North Devon District Council by the Devon Trust for Nature Conservation.

### ● The Old Railway

Construction of the line began around 1870 and from the beginning was fraught with difficulties; it was eventually opened in 1874. It suffered from an incline out of Ilfracombe of 1 in 36 and two steam engines were often used to pull trains to Morthoe Station. From time to time, even two engines were unable to manage the climb and they had to return to the beginning and start again. In 1887 the line was converted to twin-track working and the popularity increased to a peak in 1939 when at that time there were 18 down trains and 16 up trains on weekdays and 24 on a Saturday bringing many people to the holiday resort of Ilfracombe. The last steam train puffed in anger on the line in 1964 and for a while diesels took over. The line was

Above: The North Devon coastline.

reduced to a single track in 1967 and falling business brought about its total closure in 1970. The station was dismantled in 1975 and the site was sold in 1977 to Pall Europe Ltd who needed a pollution-free environment to manufacture medical filters.

## ● Ilfracombe

Ilfracombe is set between the great Iron Age castle of Hillsborough and the seven hills of The Torrs and this has controlled its development over the years. The older parts of the town are set in the bottom part of the basin and rows of guest houses and hotels climb up the surrounding slopes. It has the usual seaside attractions, and an indoor swimming pool and the Pavilion Theatre, but is not totally overrun by tourists, which suits its rather sleepy Victorian and Edwardian self. A visit to the rugged island of Lundy is possible from Ilfracombe using the MS *Oldenburg*; there are usually about four sailings a week in the summer months. It takes about $2^{1}/_{2}$hr and the total excursion lasts around 8hr. Ilfracombe Museum is well worth a visit with its collection of artefacts and photographs. There are exotic collections of material brought back to Ilfracombe by old colonial types including a coiled cobra and alligator skin. These sit side by side with items of more local interest. It is open every day through the summer (Tel: 01272 863541 for details of times).

## Starting Point:

From the car park indicated below, take the A361, then the B3231 — you will see signs for 'The Cairn'. The climb is very steep and you should leave the B3231 at Richmond Road, to carry on up the hill on the more minor road. The route starts immediately opposite the entrance to the Pall Europe depot, which is built on the site of the old railway station.

## Parking and Toilets:

Assuming that you drive into Ilfracombe on the A361 from Barnstaple, park in the first car park that you see on the left once you have entered the town. This is half-way between the start of the ride and the centre of the town. It is also possible to start the ride from the car park at the Lee Bridge end of the ride.

*Below:* Purple loosestrife lines the way.

**Distance:** 2.3 miles (4.7-mile round trip).

**Maps**: Ordnance Survey Landranger Sheet 180.

**Hills**: The whole initial section of ride is one long steady climb. Initially when you climb through The Cairn it is quite steep, but for the remainder of the ride it is gentle.

**Surface:** Once you are over The Cairn section, which is steep and has steps, the going is good with a well-gritted stone-based surface.

**Safety:** There are no safety hazards.

**Roads and Road Crossings:** None.

**Refreshments:** Plenty of choice of the seaside variety in Ilfracombe. The Slade Reservoirs provide a picturesque spot for a picnic.

**Nearest Tourist Information Centre:**
The Promenade, Ilfracombe, Devon EX34 9BX
(Tel: 01272 863001).

**Route Instructions:**

1. (0.0 miles) The first ½mile is very steep and a little difficult as there are very frequent steps across the route.

2. (0.3 miles): Descend a few steps and pass through a wooden barrier to join the old railway line.

3. (0.8 miles): Pass through a short tunnel.

4. (2.3 miles): The ride ends at Lee Bridge.

*Below:* Returning to Ilfracombe.

# THE TARKA TRAIL
*(East-the-Water (Bideford) to Barnstaple)*

Like the Ride 24, this one is also in Tarka Country and takes advantage of the excellent Tarka Trail. The ride is from Bideford to Barnstaple and opportunity is again taken to utilise the Bike Bus for the return trip. The bus can carry up to six bikes in a specially converted section at the rear, and operates every day except Wednesday. Current departure times from Barnstaple to Bideford are 1240 and 1640. For further information and confirmation of times, telephone Devon County Council's DevonBus enquiry line (Tel: 01392 or 01271 or 01752 382800). This ride could of course be linked to Ride 24 one to produce a longer distance and the Bike Bus could be used to return you to Petrockstowe.

## Background and Places of Interest

### ● Bideford

Possibly the most attractive town in North Devon, it is reached by a notable and ancient bridge from East-the-Water. The bridge dates from the 15th century and its rather irregular characteristics are due to the use of the previous wooden bridge as a framework for its construction. The timbers of the bridge were of different lengths and the arches reflected this oddity.

Over the course of its life it has been widened and rebuilt, but in 1968 there was a serious collapse when two arches at the Bideford end gave way.

### ● Instow

This was a popular seaside resort for Victorian holidaymakers. The station is now used by North Devon Yacht Club. However, the signalbox which you pass after $2^{3}/_{4}$ miles is beautifully preserved in working condition and we were lucky enough to be shown round by an old signalman who remembered the halcyon days of the Western Region with its 'Halls', 'Castles', 'Granges' and 'Kings',

*Bottom:* Easy cycling on the Tarka Trail

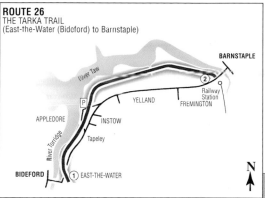

ROUTE 26
THE TARKA TRAIL
(East-the-Water (Bideford) to Barnstaple)

and who seemed to be able to talk for ever about his railway life. We all had a go at operating a signal and found it remarkably easy. However, I think that we were lucky as it is only open every other Sunday between April and September. Instow is unusual for an estuarine settlement in that it has remarkably fine sand, which contrasts with Appledore across the water, to which there is a foot ferry in the summer months. The Appledore shipbuilding industry is a latter-day success story. It is a shipyard which is very much part of the 1990s, with a covered construction area of considerable size. The North Devon Maritime Museum is sited in Odun Road and the town's long maritime tradition is portrayed in models, tools and photographs.

### ● Barnstaple

This town is the undisputed capital of North Devon and the only place in the area to have a railway station. It has the atmosphere of a county town and therefore it is surprising to find that it is only the sixth largest town in the county, but its comparative remoteness has led it to be self-sufficient over the years. It is best visited on a Tuesday or a Friday when the pannier market is in full operation. The charter for this historic market was granted by Henry II in 1272 and has been renewed by succeeding monarchs. It is one of the best surviving examples of its kind and has recently been tastefully refurbished. Stalls sell a very wide range of goods — you may even find the dark North Devon delicacy, laver bread. It is a kind of seaweed and is often cooked with bacon. Barnstaple's early prosperity involved the export of wool, and later Irish wool and yarn was brought in by boat and taken inland to factories in East and Mid-Devon. Due to silting up, this trade moved to Bideford, but even today boats call in with bulk cargoes of one kind or another.

*Above:* Barnstaple.

**Starting Point:** The old railway station in East-the-Water, Bideford.

**Parking and Toilets:** Park in the Tarka Trail Car Park in Bideford which is close to the old railway station and information centre. If you start from Barnstaple the British Rail Car Park at the railway station is conveniently situated. There is also a car park at Instow.

**Distance**: 9 miles if you use the Bike Bus to return, or alternatively an 18-mile round trip.

**Maps:** Ordnance Survey Landranger Sheet 180.

**Hills:** None.

**Surface:** A very good stone-based track.

**Safety:** There are no particular hazards on this ride.

**Roads and Road Crossings:** There is a fairly busy road to cross at Instow.

**Refreshments:** Plenty of choice at Bideford

*Above:* Instow signalbox.

and Barnstaple, but little *en route*. There are some good picnic opportunities between Instow and Yelland (3½ miles) and at Fremington (6 miles).

**Cycle Hire:** Tarka Trail Cycle Hire at British Rail station, Barnstaple (Tel: 01271 24202).

**Nearest Tourist Information Centre:** Victoria Park, The Quay, Bideford, Devon EX39 2QQ (Tel: 01237 477676/421853).

**Route Instructions:**
This is an extremely well-marked route and no directions are required. The Tarka Trail is indicated by a blue arrow with an otter footprint superimposed.

1. (0.0 miles): From the Tarka Trail Car Park at East-the-Water ascend the steps to gain access to the railway line.

2. (9.0 miles): The ride ends at the railway station in Barnstaple.

## THE CAMEL TRAIL
*(Poley's Bridge to Wadebridge)*

*Thou shalt make thyself familiar with well known local phrases like 'me andsome', 'proper job', and 'me luvver'.*
One of the mandatory instructions for cycling the Camel Trail from Bridge Bike Hire

This is a 5-mile ride along the Camel Trail from deep in the wooded countryside of the upper reaches of the Camel Valley to Wadebridge. The infant, non-tidal Camel is a lively river in a deep ravine and makes a very picturesque backdrop

to the early part of the ride. The route is very well waymarked with exceptionally good information boards along the way (provided by English Heritage and the Countryside Commission), and these give interesting information about land management of the surrounding countryside. A short ride across Wadebridge will link this ride with a further section of the Camel Trail that continues onward to Padstow. The route through the town is very well signposted. On the upper stretches of the trail there are barriers/gates that are difficult for trikes, tandems or bikes with trailers to negotiate. From Boscarne the route is very well used in the summer holiday period.

### Background and Places of Interest

● **The Bodmin and Wadebridge Railway**
The railway was opened in 1834 and as such was one of the oldest steam railways. It was originally built to carry sand from the Camel estuary inland to improve the acid clay soils of these parts. In the opposite direction travelled granite and clay destined for Wadebridge Harbour. It also carried passengers and offered day trips and excursions. The line was taken over by the London and South Western Railway in 1846. The section from Wadebridge to Padstow was laid in 1899, upon which ran the Atlantic Coast Express which became a favourite way of travelling on holiday to the West Country for many families. A very

ROUTE 27
THE CAMEL TRAIL
(Poley's Bridge to Wadebridge)

*Left:* The Camel Trail.

popular day trip was a visit to Bodmin gaol to see the public hangings.

### ● The Bodmin and Wenford Railway

A restored section of the Bodmin branch line connects passengers by steam from Bodmin Parkway on the national rail network to Bodmin General station. The round trip takes 1hr (Tel: 01208 73666 for information).

### ● The River Camel

The trail is rich in wildlife. Most British mammals are common there including fox, badger, rabbit, deer. Less common are the beloved otter and the Greater Horseshoe bat. The river supports salmon and trout and downstream, where the river is tidal, bass and mullet are to be found.

### ● Wadebridge

In 1382 the place was simply called Wade which meant 'ford' or 'a place you can wade across'.

The name came from the Old English 'gewæd'. 'Bridge' was added later, so the current name can be taken to mean 'the place by the bridge at the ford'. With this geographical setting, you would expect it to be a charming little place, and so it is. It used to be dominated by its lovely old multi-arched granite bridge, but now it is dominated by two bridges, the second carrying the A39 trunk road traffic safely around the town. It is a town of two moods. When the water is low it can be a sombre enough place, but its mood changes when the cool salt wind signals that it is time for the tide to come in and restore life to the river. Before long the tidal water is lapping around the buttresses and a flow of foamy water quickly drowns the large waste banks.

*Below:* Old Wadebridge Station — now the John Betjeman Centre.

### Starting Point:

The directions for this ride start from the car park at Poley's Bridge, which is about 5 miles due east of Wadebridge. There are many other possible starting points from the parking places outlined below.

**Parking and Toilets:** Park at the Poley's Bridge Car Park which is as at the start of the Camel Trail. WARNING: for those of you who carry cycles on a roof rack there is a headroom restriction bar at this car park and also others on the trail which at 6ft 3in (1.9m) is just the right height to knock the bikes clean off the roof.

Other car parks (and possible starting places) are at Hellandbridge, Dunmere, Grogley Halt, Polbrook and at the end of this ride at the Jubilee pay and display car park at Wadebridge. There are toilets at the Nanstallon Tea Gardens (for patrons only), and at Wadebridge (near the Swan Hotel).

TY FISHER CENTRE
ADMINISTERED BY W.Y.P.A.C

**Distance:** 11.4 miles (22.8-mile round trip).

*Above:* The easy way to do it.

**Maps:** Ordnance Survey Landranger
Sheet 200.

**Hills:** None; being a railway line the track is
fairly level. The route descends gently all the
way to Wadebridge, so there is a little bit of
work to do on the way back.

**Surface:** Excellent, stone-based with grit
dressing.

**Safety:** There are no particular hazards.

**Roads and Road Crossings:** Only one worthy
of note — the busy A389 — great care should
be taken here.

**Refreshments**: The Borough Arms alongside
the route near Bodmin. There are pleasant tea
gardens at Nanstallon immediately alongside
the route at Point 5.

**Cycle Hire:** Although private cycles are
completely free to use the Camel Trail, hired
cycles must carry a valid Camel Trail licence
disc. The annual licence helps to pay for the
upkeep of the trail. Licensed hirers are:
Bridge Bike Hire          Tel: 01208 813050
Bridge Cycle Hire         Tel: 01208 814545
Cycle Revolution          Tel: 01208 812021 &
                                        72557
Camel Trail Cycle Hire    Tel: 01208 814104
Glyn Davies Cycle Hire    Tel: 01841 532594
Park & Ride               Tel: 01208 814303

**Nearest Tourist Information Centre:**
Shire House, Mount Folly Square, Bodmin,
Cornwall PL31 2DQ (Tel: 01208 76616).

**Route Instructions:**

1. (0.0 miles): At the car park look for the
fingerpost directing you to the start of the trail.
Very few directions are necessary as the route
is well waymarked.

2. (0.8 miles): Alongside Bridge Pool Cottage,
cross a small country road.

3. (2.9 miles): Cross another quiet road here.

4. (5.9 miles): The route crosses a very busy
main road (A389); take great care here.

5. (6.8 miles): Cross a very minor road to pass
the Camel Trail Tea Gardens at Nanstallon.

6. (11.2 miles): When you reach 'civilisation',
continue along the riverbank to the multi-
arched bridge in the distance to take you to
the Jubilee Car Park which marks the end of
the ride.

7. (11.4 miles): The ride terminates at the car
park, but if you wish you can extend your ride
by a further 10.4 miles by riding the 5.2 miles
to Padstow (see Ride No 29).

# PENTEWAN VALLEY LEISURE TRAIL
*(Pentewan Village to London Apprentice)*

 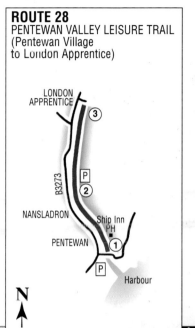

This trail is level and ideal for family cycling. It runs due north from the river bridge in the beautiful little harbour village of Pentewan and follows the St Austell River for most of the way to the village of London Apprentice. The river now runs clear as the china clay companies no longer discharge their milky-white sediment into its waters. For the most part the trail is on the edge of woodland, or runs through woodland. To the east of the trail are large areas of Woodland Trust land. The trail was opened on 31 March 1995 and was the result of much co-operation by many agencies, authorities and companies. It is ideal for family cycling — as you will see if you ride it in August — but it is also used by walkers and horseriders, so you may have to ride in single file where necessary.

## Background and Places of Interest

### ● Pentewan

The history of Pentewan is basically one of stone and clay. During the 15th century a great amount of church rebuilding was carried out in Cornwall and stone from Pentewan quarries was in demand. The discovery of clay at nearby Carloggas in the

18th century brought new work to the port. A harbour was built, but it is now silted up. It is worth going to see as it is a picturesque old place, and still has water but no access to the sea.

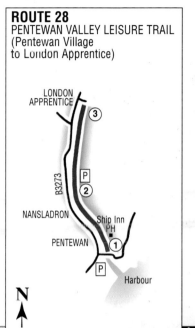

**ROUTE 28**
PENTEWAN VALLEY LEISURE TRAIL
(Pentewan Village
to London Apprentice)

LONDON APPRENTICE

③

B3273

Ⓟ
②

NANSLADRON

Ship Inn
PH

PENTEWAN

①

Ⓟ

Harbour

N

*Above:* The Pentewan Valley.

### ● Wheal Martyn China Clay Museum.

This is an unusual open-air industrial archaeology museum based on restored clay works and dates from around 1880. It has working water wheels, wagons, locomotives and a craft pottery and is situated about 2 miles north of St Austell on the A391 (Tel: 01726 850362).

### ● St Austell

A comparatively recently built town, which owes its origins to mining and china clay activities since 1750. It is a pleasant place quietly enjoying life away from the shopping precinct and rumbling clay lorries. Today, the town is the centre of the china clay industry and its many associated trades and services. English China Clay has its headquarters there. The landscape (if landscape is what you would call it) is dominated by huge tips of waste sand, which fortunately are gradually being grassed over.

*Below:* The start of the trail.

**Starting Point:** The trail starts about 200yd from Pentewan village.

**Parking and Toilets:** During peak holiday periods, parking is likely to be difficult due to the very limited parking space available. Use the free car park on the right just as you enter the village. Avoid the car park immediately by the harbour as this is limited to 1hr parking. There is an additional Woodland Trust car park over a stone bridge off the B3273 about 400 yards north of Nansladron.

**Distance:** 2.3 miles (4.6-mile round trip).

**Maps:** Ordnance Survey Landranger Sheet 204.

**Hills:** None.

**Surface:** An excellent stone-based, grit-dressed track that averages about 9ft wide over most of its length.

**Safety:** No safety problems.

**Roads and Road Crossings:** Two short sections are shared with the possibility of vehicular use.

**Refreshments:** The Ship Inn and The Cove Eating House look comfortable enough.

**Cycle Hire:** The Pentewan Cycle Hire Company operate at the beginning of the trail.

**Nearest Tourist Information Centre:** The Post Office, 4 Custom House Hill, Fowey, Cornwall PL23 1AA (Tel: 01726 833616).

**Route Instructions:**
In the summer months of July and August this is a well-cycled track used by families with very young children. It is therefore very easy cycling and very few directions are required.

1. (0.0 miles): Take the route that proceeds between wooden railings.

2. (1.2 miles): You will come across a bridge connecting the track and the B3273. There is a small car park here. Keep straight on. A small section from 1.6 miles to 1.9 miles is shared with a very quiet lane.

3. (2.3 miles): The ride terminates where it meets the B3273.

*Below:* Houseboat

## THE CAMEL TRAIL
*(Wadebridge to Padstow)*

*Is it rounding rough Pentire in a
flood of sunset fire
The little fleet of trawlers under sail?
As they stream along the skyline
In a race for port and Padstow
With the gale?*
John Betjeman

The Camel Trail is Cornwall's only traffic-free
recreational route of significant length, and
runs for about 17 miles from Bodmin Moor to
the Atlantic Ocean. This ride links with Ride
No 27 and continues along the Camel Estuary
from Wadebridge to Padstow. Wildlife abounds
here with curlew and oyster-catchers
throughout the year and flocks of golden
plover and lapwing in the winter. Little egrets
can be seen in the creeks living alongside
herons. I cycled the route in mid-August and
without doubt it was the busiest off-road route
that I have ever cycled. On the one hand it was
nice to see so many families enjoying
themselves, but on the other I found myself
wishing for just a little cycle-free cycling!

### Background and Places of Interest

● **The John Betjeman Centre,
Wadebridge**
Housed in the old railway station, this is a
small but well-presented collection of John
Betjeman memorabilia which gives an
interesting insight into the poet who loved
Cornwall, the railway, river and estuary. It
contains letters, books, household artefacts
and photographs and there is an interesting
video to watch.

● **The Museum of Historic Cycling,
Camelford**
(12 miles north east of Wadebridge)
If you are interested in cycling, this is the
place to visit, with a history of cycling from
1818 to modern times. There are over 250
cycles with an old cycle repair workshop and
tools. The first cycle oil lamp is shown and
also displays of gas, candle, battery and oil
lighting. There is a gallery of cycling pictures
and collections of cycling postcards and
greeting cards (Tel: 01840 212811 for
information).

● **Padstow**
A charming old Cornish harbour with old
sailing ships, live sea fish in tanks, good
restaurants, and old pubs. You will find
plenty of opportunities to spend your money
here.

*Above:* The Camel Estuary.      *Right:* Padstow.

**ROUTE 29**
THE CAMEL TRAIL
(Wadebridge to Padstow)

**Starting Point:** On the north west side of Wadebridge, by the A39/A389.

**Parking and Toilets:** As the A39/A389 descends into Wadebridge, there is a car park on the right.

**Distance:** 5.2 miles (10.4-mile round trip).

**Maps:** Ordnance Survey Landranger Sheet 200.

**Hills:** None.

**Surface:** Excellent, very wide and mostly stone-based with grit dressing.

**Safety:** There are no particular hazards.

**Roads and Road Crossings:** None; an extremely safe ride.

**Refreshments:** If you are lucky, in the summer months you may discover a cycle-towed ice cream container stocked with delicious Kelleys Ice Cream after about $2^{3}/_{4}$ miles.

**Cycle Hire:** There is plenty of choice for cycle hire. The following companies provide cycles and other cycling equipment on hire, and several of them are represented at the start of the ride:

| | |
|---|---|
| Bridge Bike Hire | Tel: 01208 813050 |
| Bridge Cycle Hire | Tel: 01208 814545 |
| Camel Trail Cycle Hire | Tel: 01208 814104 |
| Cycle Revolution | Tel: 01208 812021 & 72557 |
| Glyn Davies Cycle Hire | Tel: 01841 532594 |
| Park & Ride | Tel: 01208 814303 |

**Nearest Tourist Information Centre:**
Red Brick Building, North Quay, Padstow, Cornwall PL28 8AF (Tel: 01841 533449).

**Route Instructions:**

1. (0.0 miles): The route needs no directions, it is just a matter of following the Camel Trail waymarkers.

2. (5.2 miles): The route ends at the station car park at Padstow.

*Below:* The start of the trail at Wadebridge.

# THE PORTREATH TRAMROAD
*(Portreath to Scorrier)*

 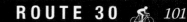

This tramroad is part of the Mineral Tramways Project that will make safely accessible the tramroads, mines and mine harbours of the Central Mining District of Cornwall. It is planned to join up this route with another one based on the old Redruth and Chacewater Railway to provide a route linking Cornwall's north and south coasts. The route is well signed; if you meet a junction with no fingerpost keep straight on, even though it appears that you are following a less-used route. Not mentioned in my instructions are the several barriers along the route that allow cycles and horses to pass but restrict powered vehicles. I found this a ride full of interest and variety. The panorama was one of hard, rather barren countryside, gaunt beam engine houses silhouetted on the skyline, crickets chirping in the grass and all this under a blazing hot Cornish blue sky.

## Background and Places of Interest

### ● Portreath Tramroad
Most tramroads were plateways — with wagons running on 3ft-long 'L'-shaped cast-iron plates. They were usually horse-drawn because the plates were too brittle to carry the weight of a locomotive. This tramroad was a single-track horse-drawn line with wagons of three tons capacity. It was developed to provide a reliable means of transport between the mines of the area and Portreath harbour and began operating in 1812. It carried goods in both directions: copper ore was sent on its way to Portreath harbour, and from there on to South Wales; coal was brought in to fuel the

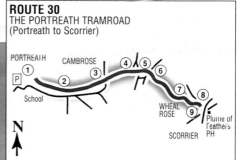

mine engines. Before the tramroads all of the ore, coal and other necessary items for copper mining had to be carried by either pack-horse or cart. The economics were simple; a horse could carry 3cwt, but a horse could tow 3 tons along the tramroad. After 1825 the tramroad experienced growing competition from railways and with the decline in copper mining in the area the tramroad ceased work in the 1860s when the last copper mine closed.

*Left:* Portreath harbour.

### ● Portreath Harbour

At one time this was one of Cornwall's busiest ports. It began operating in 1760 and its primary trade was with South Wales dealing mainly with copper ore and coal. It could never be used all the year round and it was necessary to utilise huge yards to store enough coal to supply the mine pumping engines during the winter.

*Below:* Wheal Rose.

### ● The Mineral Tramways Discovery Centre,

Groundwork Kerrier, Old Cowlin's Mill, Penhallick, Carn Brea, Redruth, Cornwall TR15 3YR
Here you can learn more about the Mineral Tramways Network and find out about its history and conservation. At the centre are exhibitions, displays, leaflets, maps and group bicycle hire. Contact them for opening hours, events programme and information on publications (Tel: 01209 612917).

**Starting Point:** Take the B3300 in the Redruth direction until the Portreath CP School appears on the right. Take the little road to the left, opposite the school, and after a few yards you will see the sign for the Portreath Tramroad clearly marked. Turn right here and commence the ride.

**Parking and Toilets:** There is a pay and display car park by the beach in Portreath, with toilets nearby.

**Distance:** 4.4 miles (8.8 mile round trip).

**Maps:** Ordnance Survey Landranger Sheets 203 and 204.

**Hills:** The outward leg is one gentle climb of about 300ft over a distance of $4\frac{1}{2}$ miles.

**Surface:** It varies between a stony uneven surface (which might be a little rough for small children), through a well-gritted stone-based route, to quiet tarmac lanes, but would appear to be good throughout all seasons.

**Safety:** At the beginning of the ride, if you have young children, you should be a little careful of the steep escarpment on the right.

**Roads and Road Crossings:** You are required to follow fairly quiet roads for short distances, but often the verge is wide enough to walk or cycle safely off the road.

**Refreshments:** In Portreath there is, as you would expect, a seaside café, the Basset Arms and many other pubs. At the end of the route is the Plume of Feathers close to the A30 at Scorrier.

**Nearest Tourist Information Centre:**
28 Killigrew Street, Falmouth, Cornwall
TR11 3PN (Tel: 01326 312300).

**Route Instructions:**

1. (0.0 miles): From the starting point opposite the Portreath CP School, proceed in the direction indicated by the tramroad sign, to begin a steady climb uphill.

2. (0.5 miles): Cross a very quiet country road to continue.

3. (1.6 miles): Just after the information plaque that indicates the passing loop, you will follow a section that follows a very quiet narrow lane. This lane joins another one and then meets a main road where you should turn left and follow it for a short distance. This road has a generous grass verge upon which you may wheel your bike if you wish.

4. (2.3 miles): Turn right off the main road to follow a quiet lane at the head of the valley. An information plate tells you that you are on an embankment and parapets built for the tramroad.

5. (2.4 miles): The quiet lane crosses a more major one.

6. (2.7 miles): Cross a very quiet little lane and then your route becomes a public bridleway. After a mile the surface changes to a white gritty and sandy nature.

7. (4.2 miles): At the declined industrial area and scrapyard — there is a residence called 'The Good Days' turn left.

8. (4.2 miles): You will come to a road where you should turn right.

9. (4.4 miles): The ride ends at the junction with the A30 Bodmin left, A3047 Redruth right.

*Below:* Portreath.

## Forestry Commission Land

The Forestry Commission (FC) was established in 1919 to ensure an adequate supply of timber for the nation's needs. At the time it was considered that the long period of time between planting and felling made this an unsuitable matter to entrust to the response of free enterprise to supply and demand. It is the largest landowner in the United Kingdom. It owns holdings of over 2 million acres and advises private owners on the management of a further million acres. Many areas of woodland owned or managed by the Forestry Commission have gravelled roads. These are well-engineered routes designed to enable timber removal by large lorries. Forestry Commission land therefore offers considerable scope for peaceful traffic-free enjoyment by the cyclist. When you are in forested areas you will see many references to 'Forest Enterprise'. This is a group within the Forestry Commission organisation.

Of course there are a great number of public rights of way on land owned or managed by the Forestry Commission and you have an inalienable right to cycle on bridleways, BOATs (Byways Open to All Traffic) and RUPPs (Roads Used as Public Paths) irrespective of who is the landowner. You must of course give way to horses and walkers on bridleways. Cycling on routes other than public rights of way can be done provided that the Forestry Commission has given permission — these routes are therefore known as permissive routes. A permissive route only exists while the landowner gives permission for use, which can in theory be withdrawn at any time.

Generally, the enlightened view of the Forestry Commission is that cycling is consistent with the use of forests for quiet enjoyment and therefore their policy is to allow cycling unless public access is restricted by title conditions or forestry operations. The precise situation will vary in each piece of woodland depending on such things as whether the commission own the land or lease it, the existence of sporting rights, the size of the woodland block and the nature of the subsoil. The situation is therefore one of a delicate balance between forestry needs, sporting needs, riding, walking and cycling.

The general rule is that you may cycle on public rights of way (except footpaths). You may also cycle on the forestry roads provided

there is no sign restricting public access — for example for sporting reasons or forestry operations — or specifically restricting cycling on, for example, a walkers' trail. An increasing number of forest areas have waymarked trails for cyclists to use. Basically, if you use your common sense, and follow the Cycle Code then you will be welcomed by the Forestry Commission. The Cycle Code is:

- Expect the unexpected. Keep your speed down.
- Remember other vehicles use forest roads as well as you!
- Give way to walkers — be friendly towards other forest users.
- Hail a horse and avoid an accident!
- Keep away from all forest operations.
- Do not pass any vehicles loading timber until you have been told to do so.
- Footpaths are for walkers only!
- Cycle with care and you can come back again!

It is fairly rare for me to become lost, but when I do it is always in forest. There are usually no distinct landmarks by which you can navigate and it is less easy to see the sun which also makes navigation difficult. So a little care is needed in the larger areas of woodland like the New Forest or Savernake Forest if you are not to run the risk of becoming totally disorientated. I would suggest that if you intend to explore a particular area of woodland and wish to plan a route using gravelled roads then you should either obtain a detailed leaflet from the Forestry Commission — if there is one available — or alternatively buy the 1:25000 scale Ordnance Survey Pathfinder map for the area.

## Dartmoor National Park

Cycling is encouraged in the national park area. The policy of the authority is to encourage cyclists to keep to public roads, BOATs and bridleways where the routes are obvious on the ground. The recommend-ation of the authority is to avoid moorland areas where rights of way are not obvious as they are quite rightly concerned about habitat preservation and erosion — it is to be hoped that their concern about damage also applies in the case of horseriders.

## Hampshire (West)

**FC1 The New Forest.** The Forestry Commission produce:
- An official route map showing the cycling routes in the forest.
- A pack providing directions and maps of five waymarked trails. (I have ridden some of these and the waymarking is generally very good indeed.)

Prices and further details from The Forestry Commission, The Queen's House, Lyndhurst, Hampshire SO43 7NH (Tel: 01703 283141).

## North Wiltshire

**FC2 Savernake Forest.** This consists of more than 2,500 acres and is leased by the Commission from the Savernake Estate Company. The public has a permissive right to cycle over gravelled roads and tracks and a very enlightened attitude toward public access exists there.

**FC3 West Woods.** This 1,000-acre site is Forestry Commission owned, situated approximately 2 miles west of Savernake Forest and has a good network of bridleways and gravelled roads.

**FC4 Collingbourne.** This 1,300-acre site is situated 8 miles south of Savernake Forest and also has a good network of bridleways and gravelled roads.

If you have any problems or require further information then please contact Forest Enterprise (Forest of Dean District), Postern Hill Lodge, Marlborough, Wiltshire SN8 4ND (Tel: 01672 512520).

## Dorset and South Wiltshire

This area has a large number of sites where cyclists are welcome although some of them are quite small areas. Those marked (P) have formal car parking areas. The remainder have bell-shaped gateway areas which are used for informal parking. Please ensure that if you park in these areas that you keep well away from the actual gates which are used for emergency and forestry operations access. In these areas there are both gravelled forest roads and other tracks and a good rule of thumb is that in addition to rights of way, any track wider than 2m can be used.

**FC5**   **Hurn (P)**
**FC6**   **Moors Valley (P)**
**FC7**   **West Moors**
**FC8**   **Uddens**
**FC9**   **Cannon Hill**
**FC10**  **Vernditch**
**FC11**  **Stonedown**
**FC12**  **Field Grove**
**FC13**  **Shillingstone**
**FC14**  **Moreton**
**FC15**  **Pallington (P)**
**FC16**  **Milton Abbas**

**FC17**  **Affpuddle (P)**
**FC18**  **Cockroad**
**FC19**  **Blackdown (Hardy's Monument)**

If you have any problems or need further information, contact Forest Enterprise (Dorset Forest District), Coldharbour, Wareham, Dorset BH20 7PA (Tel: 01929 552074/551811).

## Somerset and South Devon

In this area most of the forest blocks are small with a fragile soil type and are therefore not suitable for cycling. However, the Dartmoor National Park offers good opportunities:

**NP1 Eastern Dartmoor and the Haldon Hills.** Dartmoor National Park Authority produce a leaflet with places to cycle and describing a number of options for cycling up to a 14-mile route.

**NP2 Central and South Western Dartmoor.** A leaflet is available describing places to cycle and a circular route around Princetown and Burrator. Some sections are rather arduous and you should refer to Route 22 of this book for a full description.

**NP3 South Eastern Dartmoor.** A similar leaflet describing cycling opportunities. The authority plan to update these leaflets on a regular basis.

For further information on cycling in the Dartmoor National Park, contact High Moorland Visitor Centre, Old Duchy Hotel, Princetown, Yelverton, Devon PL20 6QF (Tel: 01822 890414).

# Cornwall and North Devon

**FC20 Eggesford Forest.** Route 21 is based in Eggesford Forest. The area has several woodland blocks. There is a waymarked cycle route from Eggesford Garden Centre. I was very impressed by the centre which is an interesting combination of conventional garden centre and a good base from which to explore the forest. There is ample free parking, restaurant information centre and cycle hire. (Tel: 01769 580250).

**FC21 Abbeyford Wood, Okehampton.** This area consists of 380 acres of woodland. There is a free car park and picnic area. The wood is on the 30-mile West Devon Sticklepath circular cycle path — leaflets available from Tourist Information offices.

**FC22 Cardinham Woods Bodmin.** This area consists of 650 acres of woodland with car park, café, and cycle hire available at Easter, Bank Holidays, Cornish school holidays and Sundays, and in June to September is open every day (Tel: 01208 74244). Opening hours are 10am–5pm.

**FC23 Grogley Wood, Bodmin.** This area consists of 260 acres of woodland with restricted parking. It is mostly coniferous and only suitable for the keen mountain-biker.

If you have any problems or require further information, please contact Forest Enterprise (Cornwall and North Devon Forest District), Cookworthy Moor, Beaworthy, Devon, EX21 5UX (Tel: 01409 221692).

This section describes the cycle routes published by local county councils in the South West at the time of writing. It also contains some routes published by district councils, but the range of leaflets is developing all the time and is not necessarily complete. Most of these routes are not traffic-free but take you along quiet country lanes. The leaflets are free unless indicated.

## AVON

*The Avon Cycleway*, a well-produced leaflet describing the 78-mile circular route clockwise from Mangotsfield, plus links to towns and cities.
*The Bristol and Bath Railway Path*, a 13-mile railway path linking the two cities.
*Off-road Cycle Rides in Avon*, a set of four leaflets. (Contact the authority for the latest price.)
*Cycle Routes in and Around Weston-Super-Mare.*
*The Malago Greenway*, Bristol to Bedminster.
Yate Cycleways.
*Cycling in Bristol*, a guide to facilities for cyclists in Central Bristol.

These leaflets are published by The Director of Highways, Transport and Engineering, PO Box 87, Avon County Council, St James Barton, Bristol BS99 7SG. Avon County Council will disappear in April 1996 and its place will be taken by four unitary authorities — Bristol, Bath Wandsdyke, North Somerset, and South Gloucester. At the close of 1995, the responsibility for the promotion of cycling in the area is still undecided.

## CORNWALL

*The Camel Trail.*— Published by the Planning Department of Cornwall County Council, County Hall, Truro, Cornwall TR1 3AY.
*Pentewan Valley Leisure Trail*, a 2½-mile route north from Pentewan
— Published by Restormel Borough Council, Penwinnick Road, St Austell, Cornwall PL25 5DR.

## DEVON

*The Plym Valley Cycle Trail.* The Taw-Torridge Estuary, a cyclists' and walkers' guide including the Tarka Trail and the Barnstaple and Bideford Coast Path and Cycleway.

*The Tarka Trail*, from Barnstaple to Braunton.
*Walking and Cycling Devon*, an overview of walking and cycling in Devon.
— Published by Countryside Department, Devon County Council, County Hall, Topsham Road, Exeter, Devon EX2 4QD.

## DORSET

*The Castleman Trailway*, from Ashley Twinning to Upton Country Park.
*North Dorset Cycleway*, a 70-mile anticlockwise route around Shaftesbury, Blandford Forum and Gillingham.
*Purbeck Cycleway*, a 47-mile clockwise route from Wareham.
— Available from Transportation and Engineering Department, Dorset County Council, County Hall, Colliton Park, Dorchester, Dorset DT1 1XJ.

## HAMPSHIRE

*Off Road Cycle Trail Pack*, a set of 12 waterproof leaflets 3-26 miles long. (Contact the authority for the latest price.)
— Available from Countryside and Community Department, Hampshire County Council, Mottisfont Court, High Street, Winchester, Hampshire SO23 8ZF.

## ISLE OF WIGHT

*Byways and Bridleways by Mountain Bike*, four leaflets covering four regions of the island. (Contact the authority for the latest price.)
— Published by County Surveyor, Isle of Wight County Council, County Hall, Newport, Isle of Wight PO30 1UD.
*Cycling on the Isle of Wight*, an inexpensive leaflet giving a wealth of information about cycling on the island.
— Published by Isle of Wight Tourist Information Centres.

## SOMERSET

*Welcome to Somerset*, a set of four cycle routes around the Somerset Levels and Moors.
*Taunton Cycle Routes*, outlines the network of urban cycleways around Taunton.
— Available from Somerset Tourism, Somerset County Council, County Hall, Taunton, Somerset.

*Cycle Round South Somerset*, a 100-mile cycle route on quiet lanes from Yeovil.

*The Chateaux of South Somerset*, eight cycle routes along quiet lanes focusing on National Trust properties. (Contact the authority for the latest price.)

— Available from Tourism and Marketing Unit, South Somerset District Council, Council Offices, Brympton Way, Yeovil, Somerset BA20 2HT.

*Mendip Cycle Routes*, a leaflet containing six family cycle routes exploring Mendip's picturesque countryside. (Contact the authority for the latest price.)

— Available from Economic Development and Tourism Section, Mendip District Council, Cannards Grave Road, Shepton Mallet, Somerset BA4 5BT.

*Circular Cycle Rides in Taunton Deane*, five cycle rides exploring the Somerset Levels, the Tone Valley, and the lower slopes of the Blackdown and Quantock Hills. (Contact the authority for the latest price.)

— Published by Taunton Deane District Council and available from Taunton Tourist Information Centre.

## WILTSHIRE

*Trails for Mountain Bikes*, gives details of byways and bridleways available to cyclists over the Marlborough Downs.

*The Wiltshire Cycleway*, a network of six possible routes around Wiltshire.

— Published by Planning and Highways Department, Wiltshire County Council, County Hall, Trowbridge, Wiltshire BA14 8JD.

*Cycling in the Wiltshire Downs*, five routes along country lanes and byways through downland scenery.

— Published by the Wiltshire Downs Project, c/o Wiltshire Tourism Project, Lackham College, Lacock, Chippenham, Wiltshire SN15 2NY.

The local county council is a good starting point to find out about the cycle routes in a particular area. A lot of cycling development and promotion work is also carried on by district and borough councils, but these are too numerous to mention individually. Some county councils are currently undergoing major reorganisation due to the introduction of unitary authorities in certain areas of high population. From a cycling viewpoint it is difficult to see this as a forward step as it will lead to a fragmentation of cycling development and promotion responsibilities.

## AVON
The Cycle Project Team, The Director of Highways, Transport and Engineering, PO Box 87, Avon County Council, St James Barton, Bristol BS99 7SG (Tel: 0117 987 4633) NB Avon County Council will disappear in April 1996 and the responsibility for the promotion of cycling has not yet been decided.

## CORNWALL
Planning Department, Cornwall County Council, County Hall, Truro, Cornwall TR1 3AY (Tel: 01872 322613)

## DEVON
Countryside Department, Devon County Council, County Hall, Topsham Road, Exeter, Devon EX2 4QD (Tel: 01392 382251)

## DORSET
Transportation and Engineering Department, Dorset County Council, County Hall, Colliton Park, Dorchester, Dorset DT1 1XJ (Tel: 01305 225085)

## HAMPSHIRE
Countryside and Community Department, Hampshire County Council, Mottisfont Court, High Street, Winchester, Hampshire SO23 8ZF (Tel: 01962 846002)

## ISLE OF WIGHT
County Surveyor, Isle of Wight County Council, County Hall, Newport, Isle of Wight PO30 1UD (Tel: 01983 821000)

## SOMERSET
Somerset Tourism, Somerset County Council, County Hall, Taunton, Somerset TA1 4DY (Tel: 01823 255036).

## WILTSHIRE
Planning and Highways Department, Wiltshire County Council, County Hall, Trowbridge, Wiltshire BA14 8JD (Tel: 01225 753641)

## CYCLISTS TOURING CLUB (CTC)
Cotterell House, 69 Meadrow, Godalming, Surrey GU7 3HS (Tel: 01483 417217). *The CTC is Britain's national cyclists' association and works for all cyclists. It provides advice, legal aid and insurance and campaigns to improve facilities and opportunities for cyclists. It publishes a very useful guide to the cycle routes in England, Wales, Scotland and Ireland that is regularly updated.*

## SUSTRANS
35 King Street, Bristol BS1 4DZ (Tel: 0117 926 8893) *Sustrans is a national charity that designs and builds traffic-free routes for cyclists, pedestrians and disabled people. It is promoting the National Cycle Network which will comprise over 6,500 miles in the four home countries, which is scheduled to be complete by 2005.*